This Is Our Story

This Is Our Story

Wendi Adelson

CAROLINA ACADEMIC PRESS

Durham, North Carolina

Library of Congress Cataloging-in-Publication Data

Adelson, Wendi.
    This is our story / Wendi Adelson.
    pages cm
    ISBN 978-1-61163-457-0 (alk. paper)
    1. Human trafficking--Fiction. I. Title.

PS3601.D4668T49 2013
813'.6--dc23   2013012668

CAROLINA ACADEMIC PRESS
700 Kent Street
Durham, North Carolina 27701
Telephone (919) 489-7486
Fax (919) 493-5668
www.cap-press.com

Printed in the United States of America
2014 Printing

This Is Our Story

Introduction(s)

Grandma always warned: never share your underwear. Mom advised: go to law school and find yourself a good husband. My husband Joshua said: write this story. I have listened to only some of the sage advice I have received over the years.

In my former life, I was a corporate lawyer with a pathetic dating record.[1] None of my clients had been forced into prostitution, as far as I knew.[2] I was a tax-paying U.S. citizen with an upright upbringing, good friends, and a reputable job. I am now what the industry calls a "public interest lawyer." Now, I know the reputation that lawyers have, and I have heard all the jokes. I have also had honest conversations with people from all walks of life about the kind of law that I now practice on behalf of some of the most marginalized and defenseless people in our communities, and it is a very different kind of practice. When I talked with my husband about writing this book, I told him that I wanted to start my part of our story on human trafficking with statistics and hard facts about statutes and international agreements, about the intersection of law enforcement, state agencies and service providers and how they fail to coalesce. My husband has convinced me, and I think rightly so, that you, as an audience, don't really want to hear about all that.[3] People are drawn in by the human dimension, he tells me, and that is what I will try to give you. I have decided to tell my story and to let my clients – and now friends – Rosa

---

1. Yes, I am a lawyer, therefore I footnote. This is how I was taught to write. I am pretty sure that before law school I didn't feel the constant need to cite to wherever I first discovered information. Now, after three years in law school and years in practice to boot, I just can't stop myself. So sue me.

2. I mean, lots of them didn't seem to have any scruples at all, but most only visited prostitutes in Vegas, far away from their cushy K street offices and comfortable houses in Georgetown.

3. If you do, well then I smell a sequel!

3

and Mila tell you theirs. Our stories are connected, but each has its own distinct origin. I really don't think that I could do their stories justice, so you will hear their thoughts, to the extent possible, straight from them.

Despite all that they have been through – and you will see that it is more than anyone should ever have to deal with – Rosa and Mila want their stories heard. They want to know that they did not suffer for nothing. Our collective hope is that you will read this book, and you will learn that the trafficking and exploitation of human beings is going on all over the world, and all over the United States. You will see just how easily this same situation could happen in your own community. We hope that if you get to know Rosa and Mila, you will see that we are three women who wouldn't have otherwise met if not for the bizarre confluence of events that led us to convene in the small and wonderful town of Hiawassee Springs. Grab some popcorn and some tissues: it is going to be quite the ride.

Origins

Chapter 1

Rosa Hernandez

Querida Diary,

Lo siento, sorry that I haven't written for a few days. I've been busy with school and chores. Seems like there is always work to do, but I guess things are no busier than they've been since my dad died. I guess you could say it's been a hard time for us, but it feels like it's always been the way it is, which is okay. We get by. Sometimes I really really miss my Papi. I miss the way he used to call me princesa and give me big big hugs when he came home from work, always with his arms full of fresh pumpkin in the fall, and Mami would make it into the most delicious pumpkin empanadas. My favorite. In the spring, he came straight from the fields, fistfuls of fresh corn for the choclo em- panadas that I love. I know Mami misses him, too, but she doesn't talk about him much. None of us do. I'm glad that I can write about him to you, and think about him. I worry that I am starting to forget. Yesterday I was trying to remember the lines around his mouth when he laughed and the crinkles around his eyes when he smiled, and I couldn't. I was trying to remember what his voice sounded like, and I couldn't. It made me so sad. I was only 12 when he died, and Maria is so little that she remembers even less. I'm grateful that I came first and that I got to have more time with Papi than Maria did.

I started school again, I am in grade 8. I really love school, but Mami says I may not be able to go for much longer. The fees are really expensive, and now that Mami has to work and Papi isn't around, I may have to work more as well. I love school more than anything and I can't imagine leaving. I understand, though, and I'll do what I have to do to help Mami and Maria. It's hard to figure out what I'll miss most. I have a literature teacher this year, Señora Martinez, and she is the best. She is tall and fair skinned and looks like a yanqui from one of those American movies. We read stories and poems and my friend Ana and I like to read the stories out loud after school and make up voices for the characters. Ana does a great yanqui voice. She puts together the accent from all of the tourists she has overheard by the church in the main square, and can imitate them well.

"Oh-lah, Cowmoe istahs?" she drawls. Ana is really funny. She makes me laugh for hours, sometimes until it makes my stomach hurt, but in that really good way. I hope that Ana and I will be friends forever, and that one day, we will live in houses with lots of bedrooms for all of our children right next door to each other.

I will really miss Ana if I have to leave school. Ana is my best friend, so I'm sure she'll share her books with me and then maybe I could learn the rest of what I need to learn to be a writer or a teacher from her. When Maria is old enough, maybe she could take on an extra job so I could go back to school. All this talk is silly for now, because I may not have to stop school at all.

Much has happened since I last wrote. I met a really special woman. I first saw her around town, and then Mami invited her into our house. She wears beautiful suits, in dark colors with shiny cloth, like she is a businesswoman or like she's trying to be elected for a position in politics, like the President's wife, Cristina Fernández de Kirchner. She has the biggest, most sparkly diamond ring I have ever seen! She has long, straight, thick and shiny black hair that she wears pinned up in a fancy pile on her head. She's also from Jujuy, although she probably hasn't lived here in a while, because her Spanish sounds different than mine, more cultured, which I bet is because she speaks English instead of Spanish most of the time.

Anyway, this woman, Señora Cuenca, came to my house, and talked to my mom and sister and me about how she became successful. She said that through hard work and dedication she went to school, graduated from university and then got another degree in business, which is like being the smartest business person ever, and now she runs her own restaurant in Miami (which is in Florida, which is in the United States). She said that she will pick two girls from Jujuy to come to the United States with her to learn the restaurant business and to live with her in her house! We would also attend school in the U.S.! Mami is excited for me to win as well because Señora Cuenca told her that I could earn up to $400 per week working at her restaurant and helping her around the house. Mami couldn't believe that I could earn that much money, but Señora Cuenca gave her $5 in American money just to show her that it wasn't a big deal to her. Can you believe it? $400 per week is more than 10 times what Papi used to make each week in the fields, even including his work on the side making leather belts. Mami could afford to send Maria and me to school for as long as we wanted with money like that. Ana and I are so excited and we are doing everything we can to be picked. We have been watching American movies and practicing English every chance we get.

Ana and I are excited about so many things about America it is hard to know where to start! From the movies, it looks like American schools don't have mandatory uniforms, so I could wear anything and any color I liked. I am going to wear nothing but purple. Oh, I hope the other kids will like Ana and me and that we'll make lots of friends. Dios mio, I'm so excited!

"Rosita, ven, y haz la cena," Luz, Rosa's mom, called her from outside, telling her to come and make dinner, as she wrestled Maria out of her dirty clothes and forced her into the makeshift shower.

"*Me voy*," Rosa called to her mom, trying dutifully to disguise her frustration at being dragged away from her writing.

Sorry Diary, I have to go make dinner.

Goodnight,

Rosa

Chapter 2

Mila Gulej

"Yeah, I'll … uh have the dumplings," the twenty-something tourist said, gesturing at the laminated menu to the picture of the meat-filled ones. "My guidebook says you gotta eat dumplings when in Bratislava." His friends agreed, their six collective eyes glancing up, down and all over me.

I smiled back as sweetly and authentically as I could muster, and for what felt like the 57th time that day I agreed, "Yes, the dumplings are a must have in my city, or anywhere in Slovakia, really. You will love them," I winked, hoping he was convinced.

"Great, we'll take three plates of dumplings and three waters" said Mr. Faded Blue Jeans. His shaggy-haired friend added, "and a side order of you," not so under his breath, hoping to elicit a laugh from his unwashed crew. Thankfully, one of his pals took a look at my reaction, punched his buddy in the leg, and told him to "knock it off."

"Sparkling or still?" I asked, already imagining the very small tip from this inexpensive meal shared by the Canadian travelers who had cleverly stitched their national flag to their knapsacks so as not to be mistaken for their less popular neighbor to the south. Who knows … perhaps they *were* American?

"Oh, we'll just drink it from the tap," said the appointed spokesperson, leaning back to the point of almost tipping over in his straight-backed chair and pleased with himself and this deal of a meal he seemed to have scored.

"We don't recommend drinking the water," I informed Mr. Jeans and his ogling friends, mentally pawing at me, half enjoying the attention if it meant a bigger tip, and half disgusted by their lack of tact.

"Well, we don't recommend paying for water where we come from. We'll take tap."

I nodded and smiled again, as sweetly as I could, enjoying the idea of the cramps and diarrhea that likely awaited this cocky group of young men.

"I'll have your dumplings and water ready in one jiffy," I called to the group over my shoulder as I balanced and raised a tray of empty wine glasses and walked away.

The group laughed, "Hey waitress," Mr. Blue jeans' friend called, emboldened by his friends, "It's *a* jiffy, not *one* jiffy," they laughed out loud, shook their heads at my inability to speak their language perfectly, clearly starved for entertainment.

I went in the back to put in their order, annoyed by their corrections. I'd like to see those boys speak a few different languages and pick up English from movies and the excerpted conversations of tourists. I sighed, wishing I were stronger by now, more used to the minor insults of strangers. Reaching down to rub the scar on my left calf that mysteriously seemed to burn whenever I got angry, I thought of my dad. The scar was a reminder of a present for my eighth birthday, when my dad felt guilty enough to come around and visit my mom and me, and to bring me a doll, something I had long outgrown by that age.

It was winter, and he took me ice skating. He held my red-mittened hand in his rough paw, rubbed raw and resistant to cold. We went so fast on the ice that day I thought we could fly, and then he dropped my hand, and I sailed to the ground, and another skater slid over my leg, cutting a deep gash in my calf with his skate. My dad refused to help me up, and I lay there for a good while, shocked and in pain, stunned that he wouldn't help me up. Instead, he skated to the side of the pond, waiting for me to come to him. I eventually did, what seemed like hours later in the mind of a wounded eight year old, and Dad told me that he dropped me on purpose, to teach me a lesson: that I could only really count on myself.

Dad made good on his lesson and never came around much again, maybe once or twice over the last nine years. Every birthday since then I wonder if he'll come around again, this December 24th. I picture him showing up, with great background music playing, and we live in a big beautiful house like the ones in those Home Alone movies, and he looks so handsome like Brad Pitt when he's making the eggnog, and he says he's sorry for not being around so much, and we all laugh and hug and sing songs about the snow. We wear brand new bulky Christmas sweaters with moose and deer prints on them in red, cream and green.

But Dad never comes around, not for my birthday, or Christmas day, or anytime really, and maybe it's best, because we, my mother and I, are probably better off without him. And anyway, those sweaters hide my figure, which means fewer tips.

"Waitress? Waitress?"

"I hear you, I come," I replied, hands burning from the plate of hot dumplings.

"Oh, I'll make you come," retorted one of the sweatshirted jokers not so under his breath, exploding with his own lame joke, exchanging high-fives and back-slaps with his buddies. Again, one of the boys noticed my expression, and told his friend he was "not cool," his gaze down in embarrassment.

"Anything else I can take for you?" I asked, trying to hide my exasperation. They shook their heads, barely attempting to muffle their laughter, and I returned to the kitchen.

"Mom, I swear, this job makes me crazy sometimes." I complained over my shoulder to my mother as I washed my sore hands with cold water from the sink.

"Patience, Mila, this is what we do, might as well stop complaining," replied my mother, tiredly. My mother Adela is precisely twenty years my senior, thirty-seven now, but she looks even older than that. This August marks her twentieth anniversary working at this same restaurant in Bratislava, an occasion she will likely not acknowledge, and definitely not celebrate.

My mother never meant to get pregnant. She had dreams of going to college, of becoming something great, maybe an engineer or a doctor. Then she met Andrej. He was older, and so handsome, with his scruffy beard, grey-blue eyes, and slightly crooked nose. He drove a motorcycle and was the closest thing to dangerous that my mother had ever seen in person. She couldn't resist. Three months after they met she was pregnant. Her parents (my grandparents), strictly Catholic, gave her an ultimatum: get married or get out. My mother left her home in Trnava and moved into Andrej's sixth floor walkup in the big city, Bratislava. She got a job as a waitress at the corner restaurant and loved Andrej the best she could. He was rarely around, claimed he had to work at the rubber plant odd hours to save for the baby. He sometimes came home smelling of other women. Three months after that, he was gone.

"I'm serious, Mama, I am so tired of these stupid boys giving me a hard time, ordering dumplings, and leaving no tip. I'm broke." I finished washing my hands and threw the dirty dishtowel down in exasperation.

"Well, Mila, maybe you should stop spending all of your hard-earned money on clothes and movies and start studying for your classes and saving for your future." Adela gave her daughter a half-smile and reached in for a hug. Mila shook her off, rebuffing her mother's attempt at affection.

"What future?" barked Mila. "Bratislava is a dead end for me. High school will be over by the end of the year, and then what? My talent is wasted here. I need to be in New York City. I need to be in America."

"America? What in the world will you do in America? You want to leave me here? I have given up everything for you. Why don't you love me?" Adela, prone to drama, threw her head in her hands, fell to the floor and began to sob.

Mila, used to the routine, knelt down next to her in the busy kitchen and rubbed her back, feeling her bony spine through her grey wool sweater. "All right, mama. Everything is okay." Adela continued to cry, unabated. Mila opted for a different tactic. "Look around you, mama, is this the life you wanted for us? For me?" Mila helped her mother to her feet while she gestured to the dark and cluttered kitchen. Adela reached out and cradled Mila's face, one cheek in each hand.

"I have always wanted better for you, Mila, better for both of us. Bratislava is changing, tourism is booming, and we are saving for you. One day, you can go to University and then after you can support us both." Mila recoiled at the suggestion, wriggling out of Adela's grasp on her face.

"No! Mom, come on already. We've been over this a thousand times. I don't want to go to University and become a doctor. That was your dream. I am going to be an actress, and you don't need university for that, but I can't be a famous actress here." Mila gestured around the kitchen, as if to underline the obviousness of her point. "New York is going to be great, and I'll make enough money to bring you there, and I will buy you the nicest clothes and the most beautiful car. We'll live in a really big, nice house and we'll own a dog that looks a little like a cute hairless rat and we'll walk together around New York and everyone will stop and stare at the famous actress and her glamorous mother and their cute little dog." Mila hammed it up for her mother, prancing around the kitchen, pretending to carry a small dog, blowing kisses to the paparazzi like she had seen in the magazines.

"Oh, Mila, you and your fantasies." Adela smiled despite herself. It had been a struggle to make a life for the two of them, but Mila was worth it. Despite everything, she was the light of her life.

Chapter 3

Lily Walker Stone

Sometimes falling in love means doing things you wouldn't otherwise do when sober. I can think of no other explanation for all the ways that I have somehow agreed to change my life since I met Joshua Stone. I have no other reason to explain how I ended up in Van Buren County, Florida, smack dab in the Florida Panhandle. For one, I now say things like "smack dab." Suffice it to say, I am not the Lily of yesteryear. I am a new Lily, with two last names, but no hyphen, because frankly, I feel fragmented enough without burdening my surname and our potential offspring with that kind of baggage.

I used to be a corporate lawyer. Maybe, like my sister Elena the nurse, you have seen enough legal dramas on television to feel like you are basically a lawyer yourself. I hate to break it to you, folks, but the legal dramas do not cover most of what the daily life is a lawyer is like. Have you ever seen document review on one of your fabulous dramas? No? Never heard of it? Document review, my friends, is where you sift through mountains of paperwork and files searching for some magic words. Sometimes it takes hours, sometimes more than a few weeks, and sometimes it means that you must take a flight to some glamorous location – like Cleveland in the middle of winter – where you will spend almost twenty-four hours a day (and night) searching through piles of boxes of more piles until you find the words you are looking for. Sure, corporate law is not all about document review. Certainly, that is just one small nugget of the daily practice. At times, I was assigned to some projects that were truly intellectually interesting, but often, let's face it, the work is a bit soul deadening. Even the high points had drawbacks. Sure, I took advantage of the free meals and tagged along to every swanky hiring lunch they offered. I gained fifteen pounds my first year at the firm.

Another great aspect of corporate law is the fine art of billing. Ah, billing. Why is this worthy of mention, you ask? I will tell you. Have

you ever broken down your day into six-minute increments? Have
you ever had a conversation like this with your mom/girlfriend/
boyfriend/husband/dog? "How was your day, sweetie?" the family or romantic relation or
pet[4] will ask, inevitably around 10 or 11 p.m., which is pretty much
what time you are getting home from work these days, since you are
not anywhere near the billable hour requirement your firm sets for
the year, and it is already October, and even this conversation is costing you time that you should be billing to make sure that your bonus
will be everything you worked so hard all year to earn.

"Well, it was productive, actually. From 9:00 a.m. to 9:06 a.m. I
researched a tort question for a car company from Germany that may
have put some defective tires into the marketplace. I did the same
from 9:07 to 9:13 a.m. At 9:14 a.m. I went to the break room to get
a cup of coffee. I then used the bathroom and returned 8 minutes
later. At 9:22 a.m. I resumed research on the tort question and
then ..." Really? Do you think an actual conversation would get that
far before your loved one (human or animal) rolled over in disgust?

After more than six years at the law firm, I was fairly disgusted
with myself as well. Like legions of other young overachievers, I entered law school with dreams to change the world, provide a voice for
the voiceless, save the seals, fight injustice, la la la. After soaking up
over a hundred thousand dollars of debt at my fancy pants law school,
I decided to trade in my values and principles for a chance to get out
of debt sometime before 32, the age when I imagined I would be
grown up enough to have children and a husband.

A few months after I turned 34 and long after I'd traded in my
ideals for my comfortable corporate salary, Josh and I met at a mixer
for young professionals in D.C. and hit it off from the first minute.
He was everything I never knew that I was looking for in a guy and

---

4. Yes, I know that, as a whole, most animals do not talk, save for the very
intelligent parrot. Be that as it may, when you live alone and were putting in the
kind of hours that I was at work, I actually had an imaginary dog (the cleanest
variety) that would talk to me when I got home. Don't you dare judge me.

most of what I was already hoping to find.[5] He is my same height, which is something I had never considered pre-Joshua, because I had already determined that my dating window extended only from 6 foot two to 6 foot 4. Still, I thought this one was funny, sweet and smart enough to give a shot, despite the fact that I could never wear heels around him.

We fell in love, got hitched, and less than three months later, in early August, we moved to Hiawassee Springs, Florida. August is a time in the Panhandle when you can't move an inch outside without sweating through your shirt. It's uncomfortable, to say the least. We moved to this Godforsaken place for Josh's career, and because I wanted and needed to be with him, no matter where we were. Josh had three weeks to prepare before the semester began at North Florida State University (NFSU).[6] He finally finished his eight years of PhD and post-doc and writing fellowships and would finally be an Assistant Professor of English at NFSU, and I was going to study for the Florida Bar exam and look for a job. We had a plan. We were on our way. The thing about plans, though, as my grandmother used to say, is that we plan and God laughs. My dad also says, and I am pretty sure that he borrowed this from someone famous, that life is what happens when you are busy making other plans. Platitudes aside, all of that is to say, things happened much differently than we ever planned.

So, here we are, in Hiawassee Springs, Florida, "America's friendliest town." It turns out that another town close by is actually named the friendliest, but Josh and I insist they got it wrong, and that Hiawassee Springs was robbed of its deserved moniker. People in the 'wassee are the kind that would run through traffic if you asked them

---

5. Also, it helps that I was absolutely sick and tired of dating. I see dating, at its best, as nothing more than a romantic interview. "Are you the kind of person who would produce good looking, smart and nice children and never cheat on me and help me clean up the kitchen and love me even when I'm grouchy and not trade me in for another younger model and not join the other team?" That is always question number one. Unsurprisingly, I rarely had the men folk stick around for the second question.

6. Go Fighting Manatees!

to.[7] How did we get here? Let's see, for our honeymoon, we took the scenic route from Washington, D.C., through the Carolinas, with a mandatory stop in the not-to-be-missed *tres romantique* town of Charleston. All those cobblestones and horse-drawn carriage rides through town, I mean, it's enough to make anyone fall in love right then and there. Ten or so hours later, having seen all the back roads in the Southeast seaboard, and one very expensive speeding ticket later,[8] Josh and I arrived in Hiawassee Springs. It was pouring rain, which was just as well, because it obscured the fact that Hiawassee Springs was, shall we say, less than I had expected. It's my own fault, really, not having done enough research. I just assumed, and we all know what assuming does, that Hiawassee Springs was in Florida, and would be just like other parts of Florida that I knew from visiting my grandparents. I assumed there would be palm trees, and the beach, and sunburned Canadians, and that North Florida was basically just like South Florida. *Lily, Lily, Lily.* I definitely found out how wrong you can be with assumptions. Still, I have Josh, we have our health, and I like to think I have a good sense of humor about life. Turns out I have a good sense of humor, but only about other people's lives. I am quite humorless about my own, or at least I was. Hiawassee Springs changed everything.

First lesson: North Florida is very different from South Florida. This statement is worth emphasizing, lest other people make the same mistake that I made.[9] North Florida is much more like South Georgia, which makes sense, given its proximity. Palm trees are not native to North Florida. Some palm trees do grow here, but nature did not intend for it to be a tropical paradise in the Panhandle, or the Big Bend, as some of the locals call it.

---

7. Again, a figure of speech. I mean, the folks here are kind enough that they would go the extra mile, but we aren't the kind of cruel people who would ask anyone to run through traffic, especially not for our own amusement.

8. The nice officer told us that just two more miles over the speed limit, and Mr. Josh Speedster-Magee would have spent the night in jail. Obviously, we hadn't yet arrived at "the friendliest town" when said incident occurred.

9. I mean, this book should be first and foremost educational, no?

Next lesson: Not only is the geography different, but Hiawassee Springs is not the West Palm Beach or Hollywood, Florida that I had experienced with my grandparents. Most significantly, there is no shuffleboard here. Not even one shuffle or one board. There aren't so many Canadians either, with or without sunburns. There are, however, lots of really nice people, almost painfully so. My first few days in Hiawassee I kept getting lost, which is surprising, since it's pretty much a one traffic light kind of town. The sad truth is that my sense of direction is just that bad. Josh offered to buy me a GPS device for my birthday, so that he could track me down and give me directions if needed, but I politely declined. With me out of work and him not exactly raking it in as an English professor, I didn't want him splurging on unnecessary gifts for me. So, as I proceeded to get lost around what I am still sure is America's friendliest town, people actually stopped in the middle of the street, asked me where I was going, and then got in their cars or trucks and escorted me in the right direction. They then turned around, back to where they came from, since they were not headed in my direction themselves, but wanted to make sure I got where I needed to go. This was definitely not South Florida, or the northeast. This, my friends, is Hiawassee Springs.

Chapter 4

Rosa

December 1, 2004

Querida Diary,

You are not going to believe this, but Señora Cuenca chose me! She chose me and Ana! Out of the whole class of thirty-two students she chose us! I think it's because of our essays. We were asked to write about "Why we want to work and study in the United States of America." I wrote about how I need to take care of Mami and my sister now that my dad is gone to heaven, and how it would make our lives easier if I could go to America and learn a skill and bring money home. I have always been the best in my class in writing and well, I "helped" Ana write her essay to Señora Cuenca as well. I wrote hers about the "flora and fauna of Florida." One of the tourists once dropped a guidebook on Florida and I learned a good bit about Floridian wildlife from reading the captions under the pictures (and translating the English with a Spanish/English dictionary at the Jujuy library).

Is that wrong? I wonder if it was unfair to write Ana's essay for her since we got picked over the other students. But everyone else here reads off each other's papers and works on problems together, so it seemed okay to write something for my best friend so we could have an adventure together, right? Ana is a lousy writer and never would have made it otherwise. I just had to help her and we had to go. Maria is going to be so so so so so so jealous!

Maybe it was wrong, but anyway, I did it and it's done and we were selected! There is so much to do over the next month. Señora Cuenca wants us to move into her home by the beginning of January so we can get used to life in the U.S. and the restaurant before school starts again for the spring term. Ana and I are going to celebrate Christmas with our families and then off we go to Florida! Mami is going to make some nice skirts and tops for me for my present for la Navidad and then I will have nice things to wear in America. Once I am there I will have lots of money, and I can buy store-bought clothes for Mami and me, and maybe Maria, too, if I have enough left over.

I mean, it's okay that I wrote Ana's essay so we could win together, right? I hope Jesus forgives me. I know it is a sin to lie, and I am a good girl, but I almost never do anything bad, but Diary, you know that I tell you all of my thoughts, good and bad, because I don't want the rest of the world to know about what I did. Please forgive me, Jesus, for I have sinned. I am usually not a sinner, as you know, and I will try to make it up to you, by honoring my mother and my Papi in heaven when in America. I will try so hard at school, and I will be the best girl when I am with Señora Cuenca, and I will work very hard in the restaurant, and I won't spend any money on myself: everything will go home to take care of Mami and Maria so Mami won't have to work so hard. I promise, I will redeem myself in America.

Amen,

Rosa

Chapter 5

Mila

I need to get the hell out of Bratislava. I don't want to end up like my mom. Don't get me wrong, I love her, and I know she's doing the best she can. It's just that I see her, and I think, wow, is this it? Sometimes I wonder whether it would be better just not to know, you know? I wish that I wouldn't meet so many tourists, or see movies from the U.S., or read magazines or anything. Then, I really think I could be happy with what I have, instead of wishing I were somewhere else, living a different life. I mean, I get it. I'm almost eighteen years old already, not a child anymore. I've lived enough years and seen enough things to know that things aren't always what they seem. I know that life anywhere isn't like what you see in the movies. Still, I can't help but think if I just made a change, a big change, to somewhere better than here that things would turn out different and better for me than they did for my mom.

I have a new guy in my life. Marek. He came to the restaurant about a month ago one Thursday evening and nervously ordered coffee after coffee until the place closed and then left a hefty tip and his number on a napkin. I took the tip, but I never called. He came back about two weeks ago and repeated the same coffee overdose except this time we started to talk. Out of total boredom I went home with him that night. Now we're seeing each other. He's like everything else here. Nice, but ordinary. With him, it feels like I am sitting in a closed box where I feel the air and possibilities slipping away. Even the sex is nothing special, not exciting.

Last week, after a particularly boring Sunday afternoon, I was reading the paper at Marek's house while he fixed a broken stair leading up to his boring fifth floor flat. I saw an ad in the paper for restaurant workers in New York City. They want people who are familiar with Chinese food and know how to work hard. It made me think, you know? I mean, I work in a restaurant here, and I live with my mom, so my expenses are low, so it would seem like it would make more sense to stay put, and try to save for the future. And yet, something about that ad really draws me, makes me want to take a chance. I could be working in New York City, where a famous agent or actor could see me clearing plates of pork fried rice and just know that I could be the next big thing. I'm excited by the possibility.

I know my mom is never going to let me go and be a dishwasher or a waitress somewhere far away when I can do that here. Maybe I won't tell her. Maybe I'll tell her that Marek got a raise and so we are taking a vacation to the big city. Or I could tell her that Marek works at a travel agency part time and that he won the award for the most sales last year and so he won a free trip anywhere and we are choosing New York City. It doesn't really matter what I tell my mom, it just has to be a lie good enough that she'll believe it.

I know she wants the best for me, and this just isn't it. I can't breathe here. I have to respond by the 9th of this month. That gives me six more days to decide between my mom and Marek and the life I've known here, and anything that might possibly be in New York City. Who needs six days? I'm out of here.

Chapter 6

Lily

So, I quickly learned that North Florida would not be what I had expected. I found myself waking up each morning, repeating to myself, "Lily, everything is okay. You love Joshua, and you chose this change. You are not a victim." Josh definitely helped, or tried to. He found a website called "Morethanyoumightthink.com" and would send me little clips from its bounty of cultural wonders available for viewing and attending in Hiawassee Springs. Our conversations went something like this:

"Hey Lily, I have a great idea. Let's go to the Hiawassee Springs Museum on Thursday night for a sewing group or we could go to a watercolor class at the local community college this weekend. It might be fun." It might have been. I tried, I went to the sewing party, and it turns out, you really needed to know how to sew beforehand. I guess that makes sense.

Not one to handle free time well, I took a job with the local Immigrants' Justice Center of the Big Bend (IJC). Much like other decisions I made once we decided to move to the Panhandle, I am not sure what inspired the choice. I think my past desires to do some kind of do-gooder law had long been squeezed out of me by law firm life. I didn't have a particular interest in immigration or immigrants,[10] but

---

10. Maybe that is not entirely accurate. My mother is actually from Buenos Aires, Argentina, and her parents were originally from a country that no longer exists somewhere in the former Austro-Hungarian empire, now modern day Poland or possibly the Ukraine. They left Argentina when *Mami* was in her late teens — when my grandparents felt the stirrings of dictatorship, they took their daughters to the United States, and wanted them to be as American as possible to keep them safe. They celebrated *Mami*'s marriage to a blue blood American guy like my dad, James Daniel Walker. I digress. I recognize now that I am the child of an immigrant who is descended from immigrants, but none of this resonated with me at the time.

I had heard people on TV and the radio (and my cousin Hal who un-fortunately is a blood relation) rant and rave about illegal immigrants for quite some time. Between you and me, when I signed up for the job, I didn't know the first thing about immigration law. Mainly, I just needed a job to occupy my time, and it was basically the only one available just then. Type A personalities like mine don't really jibe well with free time. Shouldn't we always be doing *something*? I had made a good bit of money at the law firm, but we had spent most of my savings on the wedding and the move. I suppose I could have sat around and done absolutely nothing for at least a few months, given the low cost of living in the Big Bend, but

1) I hate it when I don't have anything to do[11] and
2) Josh still had gobs of loans to pay off from his many years of graduate school.

So, I sent my resume around and found the first place that would hire me: the IJC. I quickly realized that I would be the only immi-gration lawyer – for a span of about 300 miles – providing free legal services. Day one proved that while I had gone to law school and had already represented a handful of big, important corporations,[12] I did-n't know squat about immigration law, and there wasn't another lawyer around for miles and miles to teach me. So, I decided that rather than rely on the IJC's malpractice insurance[13] and just have a go at it, I would sit down during the fabulously free nights that Josh and I had in Hiawassee Springs, and just start learning.

It definitely took more than a few months to come close to any-thing I would call competent, but I started to make heads or tails of what legal remedies existed for immigrants who found themselves in North Florida. I was ready for business.

First, I had the drop ins, the people doing construction around town who saw the shingle we hung outside that read "Free legal serv-

---

11. Aside from make numbered lists, that is. I love numbered lists, and bul-let points, and making lists about the kind of lists I like to make.

12. None of which actively clubbed baby seals or drowned kittens in the local river, as far as I know.

13. And, to be honest, the fact that my impoverished and basically non-Eng-lish speaking clients were unlikely to sue me.

ices" in English and Spanish and decided our help was in their budget. I met young men of all ages from many different countries in Central and Latin America who just could not get over the *gringa* who spoke Spanish. No matter how many times I told them that my mom's family was from Argentina, and that my maternal grandparents basically raised me while my mom was working, they just could not believe it.

"*Pero, eres tan blanquita.*" But you are so white, they would say. "*Y tambien, eres tan joven.*" But you are so young, how could you be a lawyer already? How do you know Spanish again?

I cannot overemphasize how much I enjoyed this constant assertion, no matter how false it might be, that I could not possibly be old enough to be a lawyer. Some of them were at least ten years younger than me, but lives lived outside, doing construction, picking fruit, chasing dreams on this side of the border: these things harden the shell a bit, make the skin a little less supple. Comparatively speaking, both to my clients and to the rest of the world, I had lived a life of outrageous privilege and unfathomable comfort. My hands have never worked a day of hard labor, unless you count the kind that worsens your glasses prescription and gives you that special shade of green/pale that only a Caucasian in a cold climate toiling in artificial light can achieve. Sure, I billed lots of hours at the firm, but only because I had the luxury to go to law school, three years where I did not have to support a family, or work outside or alongside dangerous machinery in a meat-packing plant to barely make a go of it. The closest I had gotten to actual hard work – until just about now – is the time I had spent volunteering at soup kitchens, where jobs aren't always easy to come by, but are a means of putting food on the table, not the culmination of years of graduate school focused on one's personal academic passions.

After I had met with a few clients who spread the word (and word travels faster than a stallion in heat in these here parts),[14] I started receiving many referrals from different organizations in town. One such

---

14. I admit, that isn't actually something people say here, but maybe it should be.

source was the local Mormon church. These folks were really nice, and meant well, no question. First, there was Bob. Bob called because his young friend from church, Jorge, wanted to become an American citizen and to bring his family over from El Salvador. Bob thought that Jorge might have a claim on citizenship because his family was being threatened by gangs. Now, I had never done an asylum case based on gang threats, but I was excited for the challenge. I set up an interview with Jorge, and Bob showed up with him. I kindly showed Bob to the waiting area,[15] but he persisted.

"Jorge is my friend and I want to make sure that you, little lady, are doing everything you can to do right by him." Bob said, as he hooked his thumbs into his worn blue jeans, and I kid you not, he tipped his hat to me as he said the words "little lady." Legal ethics and Professional Responsibility taught me squat about the practice of law in the Panhandle. I fought every urge I had to swift-kick that Mormon cowboy right in his set of holy plates.

Instead, I calmly replied, "Now Bob, Jorge and I are going to have a little talk in Spanish, and I wouldn't want you to feel left out. Just have a seat here by the magazines. Oh, look, we have a copy of the latest Fish and Stream! Enjoy!" And with that, I quickly closed the door to the waiting room/porch, turned on the heel of my non-heeled foot and headed back into my office where Jorge, sweet, non-English speaking Jorge, was patiently waiting.

Jorge and I had a good conversation about his life experiences back in El Salvador. He was in a gang for many years, had lots of tattoos with bullets and naked ladies on his arms, and he had done lots of things that he was not proud of at all. Then, in the last year, he snuck across the border, came to Hiawassee Springs, met Bob and found Jesus.[16] It sure seems like 2004 was a very busy year for Jorge. Given

---

15. Lest you get any grand ideas about the ICJH, let me clarify. This "waiting area" is actually the porch outside. There are two chairs, one of them has a back but tilts forward at an awkward angle, and the other has arms but no back: it's your choice. There are magazines, but sometimes they get a little sticky from the humidity, or the jam-covered hands of my clients' kids. Either way, that is our waiting room in all its glory.

16. All in that order.

that Jorge spoke no more than 9 words of English, I suppose that he was able to communicate "gang" to Bob, which Bob must have thought was what Jorge feared, and not what Jorge was part of. Minor distinction.

I kindly explained to Jorge that our funding prevented us from taking on any case in which a client had committed a crime. He said that he understood, that it was a pleasure to meet me, and gave me a polite kiss on my right cheek, Latin style, and we went to meet Bob in the waiting room.

"How could you be done, already? It's only been twenty minutes, Miss Lily!" Bob reeled at the possibility. "I think maybe I'd best stay out here a while, while you and Jorge continue to have a little talk." He stood in the doorway and gave Jorge a nudge back inside.

"Bob, I am grateful that you have been such a good friend to Jorge, but he is not going to be my client. He understands and I understand. I will see you around." I kindly, but with just enough gusto, gave them an expedited ushering out the door. Jorge never called again, but Bob called, just about every Monday morning, after seeing Jorge in church over the weekend, with new possibilities for Jorge's immigration status.

Without fail, each Monday Bob would call and always assume that I knew it was him, which I did. "Miss Lily, could Jorge claim asylum because of religious persecution?" I explained that unfortunately for Jorge, you had to actually be persecuted on account of your religious beliefs to qualify for asylum based on religious persecution. Crazy, huh.

The following Monday, "Hey Miss Lily, could I adopt Jorge?" Bob asked, earnestly, and without the slightest bit of humor. I kindly explained that Jorge was 26 years old, and that for immigration purposes, he was too old to adopt in order to change his citizenship.

You had to give him credit: this Bob was both kind and creative. I haven't heard from him lately and sometimes I wonder if it's because he skipped town to go to law school somewhere.

Transitions

Chapter 7

Rosa

Querida Diary,

There is so much to say. I am afraid that if I don't write it all down, that I will think everything has been a dream, and I will forget it all. Writing has always been the way that I understand my world. I am afraid that if I stopped writing I would lose every last shred of Rosa and then there would be nothing left. I don't want to forget everything that has happened, but maybe bits and pieces will fade after a while, and that will be okay, too. It has been a few months since I last wrote, but it might as well be ten years. Everything is totally different now. Ana is gone. We are both gone, but Ana is really gone.

Where do I begin? Señora Cuenca arranged for us to have tourist visas, and she decided that it would be easier for everyone if Ana and I wrote "Cuenca" as our last name on the passports, so that the Immigration People would think we were a family and not give us any trouble. At the time, I couldn't believe how nice she was about everything. Apparently it cost about $4000 U.S. to bring us both over to Miami and the Cuencas have paid for everything for us. Their generosity made me want to work even harder for them.

Before we left, I had the nicest Navidad together with my family. All of my aunts and uncles and cousins were there, and we played music and danced until four in the morning! I couldn't stay up and nodded off around two, but everyone else just kept going. Mami made

all of my favorite food and we had this beautiful almond cake that
Mami made for everyone, shaped like Florida, to celebrate my big trip
to America. Everyone was really proud of me and excited for me.
Maria was mostly excited because she won't have to share a room with
me anymore, but secretly I think she'll miss me.

   Diary, when I write to you now, Navidad seems like a very long
time ago. After the celebrations, Ana and I packed our things and got
on a very long bus ride from Jujuy to Buenos Aires, which is the capital
of Argentina. We stopped a lot and it took about two days to finally arrive (the bus kept breaking down, and we needed to stop every few
hours for sodas to pass around the bus, and maté breaks in the afternoon, of course). We took another bus from the bus station to get to the
airport. I wanted to see so much more of Buenos Aires, but it was hard
to make out most of it from a bus window, with the city whizzing by
at millions of kilometers each minute. Every once in a while we would
stop at a traffic light, and I would wave at the people on the street
(Ana gave me the window seat, she said she preferred the aisle. Really, though, I think she wanted to show me in little ways how grateful she was to be going on this trip with me). When we finally got to
the airport, we were really tired and dirty, but we had a few hours to
clean up and prepare for our flight. We had the most fun in the airport bathroom, trying to wash up with the sink soap and then drying
off with these machines that turned on and off and somehow can tell
when parts of your body are underneath them. I swear we ran in and
out of those machines, splashing water on each other and then drying
off, for hours.

   Ana and I had never been on a plane before, and it really was
amazing. Way more amazing than even those cool dryers in the bathroom. We read through all of the safety materials to ensure that in
case of an accident, we would be prepared. The announcements were

made first in Spanish, then in English, and I strained to make out a few words in English. "Life vest," that one I could tell from context. I practiced each word out loud and committed it to memory. "Lie-f best." I said each word three times and then it became my own, just like Señora Valdez taught me in language class. "Emergency exit." That one was accompanied by the flight attendant lady's bizarre hand motions all over the plane. Ana took out the paper bag in the front of her seat, and two minutes later, she had turned it into a frog puppet. Ana always made me laugh so much.

Ana. Ana. Ana. Everything is so wrong now. I can still see her, clear as life, in front of my closed eyes. She is laughing, making ribbit sounds with her frog puppet. We were so excited for everything that would come. There was no way for her to know that things would be so terribly different from anything we could have imagined.

That plane ride seemed to last forever, but really, it was only about eight hours long. We realized, when the plane touched down, that this adventure to America was really going to happen, and we held each other's hands and gave out a little squeal: We couldn't believe our good luck!

We un-boarded the plane and got ready to see Señora Cuenca again. We bounded off, arm in arm, ready to take on America. We got through customs with our rehearsed statements. We said that we were sisters, Ana and Rosa Cuenca, coming to Miami to visit our Aunt Patricia, and to help take care of our new baby cousin, Daniela. We had each secured a tourist visa for the trip and would go to school with our cousin, who was our same age. We repeated this story three times to the different immigration people and the customs people and they let us through. Repeat it three times and it's yours.

We passed through a hall of glass walls and saw lots of excited people and were released into the regular airport space. There was a large family of people with skin my color wearing the most beautiful clothing, women with long, black wavy hair wearing gold and green and purple holding a sign that said "Singh." I wanted to tell them that they spelled it wrong. I thought they might want my help. Ana thought better.

The crowd of faces of families and friends waiting for everyone that got off the plane was thick with people. I panicked, unsure if I would be able to remember Señora Cuenca. I scanned the crowd once, then twice, and didn't see her. Ana did her best to reassure me with her frog puppet, who she named "Prince," but I started to get really scared. What if no one showed up to meet us? We would be all alone in America, Ana and me. Just then, Ana had Prince tug at my arm.

"She's right there!" Ana shrieked.

I still couldn't see her, my eyes scanned the crowds until I saw that signature hairdo. Bingo. Except, instead of her hair looking stylishly piled on her head, Señora Cuenca looked like she'd just been through a wind tunnel.

I'll write more soon, Diary. I'm too tired for more tonight,

Rosa

Chapter 8

Mila

I left. Just like that. I did it. Well, not just like that. Making a decision is like snapping your fingers. You decide and it's done. The process of carrying out your plans takes longer.

The first lie was to my mother, that I had a job as an au pair lined up in the States. The second lie was to Marek, that I would be back in six months and we would pick up where we left off. I knew then that even if I were back in six months, that I couldn't spend one more minute with Marek. Terribly, awfully nice Marek, with his short well-behaved hair, clean white t-shirts and acid wash blue jeans that were suddenly popular in Bratislava but that probably went out in the 1980s in America. That's where I was going. America.

I answered that ad I saw in the paper about the Chinese restaurant. The number linked to a city called Atlanta, which is in the southern part of America. I had never heard of Atlanta before, but the agency reassured me that it was close enough to New York, and that I could still visit and go there on my vacations with all the money I would make at the restaurant. The agency in Atlanta said that they would place me with a Chinese restaurant that needed help, they would arrange for my work visa, and that I could be on a plane within two months. Finger snap of a decision: I said yes. Yes, yes and yes. I was on my way.

The next two months passed quickly. More lies to my mother, more lies to Marek. My mother was sad about my leaving. She would hold on to me a little past loving, to make a fleeting hug last longer than it should, longer than it could given that I was already one foot out the door.

I felt selfish. I know that I was all she had, other than that stupid job I couldn't wait to leave. The restaurant was not enough to live for. At least for me, it wasn't enough of a future to sit around waiting for. My mom had already had her time to be young, and this was mine. As long as I could make it to the States, even if it was Atlanta and not New York, it was a step in the right direction. I was heading toward something un-known. I wanted this change, and I needed this change, to take my life's direction in my own hands and steer it. I was on my way.

The agency paid for my ticket. I would first take the train from Bratislava to Vienna, then fly to London, then Miami, then Atlanta. How I wished that I could stop at each of those places I had never seen! I bet if I could just wander around the big cities like Vienna or London, or stroll around in my bikini in Miami that I would defi-nitely get discovered! Sadly, without that extra time and money I would have to head straight to Atlanta to the restaurant, and begin my real professional life after. I cannot complain, really. The agency also arranged for my housing, a nice apartment right above the restaurant (which was great, because apparently Atlanta's public transportation system did not reach the part of the city where the restaurant and the apartment were located).

There I was: I had a ticket, a visa, a place to stay and a place to work. All that remained were some goodbyes. I worked my last shift at the restaurant on a Saturday night, even though I had a very early flight Sunday morning. Who cared? I could sleep on the planes.

I wore something extra low-cut for my last shift, despite the weather, hoping for some extra tips from the tourists. I worked along-side my mom, and the time with her, the quick moments of shared grief over a low tip or having her help me rub out a fresh stain caused by a sloppy soup eater felt more special than usual. My mom, the other restaurant workers and I toasted my last night with the rest of a bottle of red wine that some American tourist had ordered, tasted, drank half the bottle, and then decided that it "didn't suit his taste." Sigh. Americans. Always with so much left over. They use something, and then they just want to toss it out with the garbage. Either way, they prefer not to pay.

I bid a quick goodbye to my mom and promised to be home soon to spend what was left of our last night together in Bratislava. I took the bus to see Marek, who, at least for boring Marek, seemed quite devastated that I was leaving.

"You will come back, I will see you in six months, yes, Mila?" He said it more like a pleading statement, less like a question, like he al-ready knew that I would rather stay in Atlanta than with him.

"Marek, I told you, the visa is only for six months. I can't stay a minute longer even if I wanted to."

"I know you want to," he said, in a weak attempt to look cute. Poor Marek, with his oversized gaunt head and protruding beak-like nose, just couldn't pull off cute.

I tried to reassure him that I wanted to stay and be with him. It seemed like the right thing to do, to lie to him, given his state of sadness. Marek, though, was a little more intelligent that I gave him credit for. He knew we were over, just as I knew we were over, and, after a long, lingering kiss, we hugged goodbye. It felt like saying goodbye to a random classmate for the summer on the last day of school, not caring a bit if you saw them next year. Either way, I was out the door forever.

Humming "Welcome to Miami" by the American musician Will Smith in my head and out loud, I bounded off the bus, skipped down the street and bolted up the stairs to see my mother. I found her in bed, curled into a fetal position and sobbing softly, her small frame shaking a bit with each cry. I took off my shoes, and without undressing, molded into her back, and firmly placed my arm around her waist.

"This is your safety strap, mom. You always told me, 'Safety first!'"

She chuckled despite herself. "Stop that, Mila, don't you dare make me laugh. I'm sad. I'm allowed to be sad."

"Not while I'm still around, and mom, I'll always be around. Just as soon as I can I'll be sending money to you and saving more money and as soon as I can get you to New York, we will start living right."

"Get some rest, Mila, you have a long day of travel ahead. I love you, my little girl. Close your eyes and sleep."

The truth was, I couldn't have slept if I tried. I was way too excited to travel all the way to this placed called Atlanta. I knew that when I woke in the morning, I would be on my way to an entirely different life.

Chapter 9

Lily

Yesterday I met with some new clients. The process of interviewing and taking down information from new clients is called "intake." During yesterday's intake, I met with some nice people from Iran. As I sat with my prospective Iranian clients, I was simultaneously dumbfounded and amused: how did this young woman from Tehran, with her aunt translating and mother in tow, end up in Hiawassee Springs, Florida? How did I end up here as well? How did these people and I meet ... in Hiawassee Springs of all places ... and end up in the same place and time to be having this conversation? I never would have expected it, but this small town is packed with people from all over the world, from many different cultures and religions. If the 'wassee exists as a microcosm of the world's population, it really makes me wonder, is there even such thing as a small town anymore?

As a corporate lawyer, I never heard the juiciest bits of people's lives. You have to be at a more senior level for that, or have the time or the audacity to bill your clients for minutes stolen reading trashy gossip rags online. Here, I get to hear the tell-all version in real time. When representing immigrant women in divorce cases, I have learned a lot about erectile dysfunction and why some cultures believe that "sport" or strong tea might cure this "horrible deficiency." It is always morethanIwouldhavethought.com. All the time. I am really starting to love this job.

Other parts of life in Hiawassee Springs I love a little less. Here's an illustrative example of how, for all its richness in human diversity, this place still has lots of small town "charm." Yesterday, I got home at a decent hour and Josh had plans to spend the evening with some other English professors listening to a reading at The Plant, a local hangout for English professors and English majors.[17] Josh always invited me

---

17. ... and the folks who wanna-get-in-the-pants-of-the-English-majors.

along on these Tuesday night adventures, but in truth, sometimes I really relished the silence of a little time alone. When you are single, you want to be married, to have that special constant companionship. Then, you get married, and you miss the alone time you used to have too much of. Happy, I guess, is somewhere in the middle.

So, there I was, relishing some pre-marriage type alone time. I was sitting on our broken, deformed couch, hoping to catch a few minutes of a *Gilmore Girls* rerun. We had a television that only played three channels, and I found what turned out to be one of the first episodes of the *Gilmore Girls* on TV one afternoon. The reruns were playing every night at 7 p.m. Two episodes in and I just couldn't get enough of Lorelei's crazy antics and Rory's sensitive intelligence.

I had just sat down on the couch with a bowl full of Thai spiced noodles when I heard a scratching sound in the wall, near the base of the couch. The sound was loud, and I thought about it for a bit, but then dismissed the sound as likely coming from our porch, which was adjacent to the wall. In the last three days alone I had seen a rabbit, a squirrel and a fox[18] right beyond our porch. The scratching sound could have come from any one of the three. Who cares? It was time for my show, and noodles in hand, I turned back to hang out with the Girls.

Scratch. Scratch. Scratch Scratch.

There it was again. Shoot. This demanded some actual attention. I got up from my noodles, the couch and the Girls to inspect the wall. I looked more closely at the wall and discovered that the space in the wood-paneled wall was more than just a small opening. Yes indeed, some little critter had gnawed that crack right into a gaping hole. At that moment, I saw some kind of little animal arm crawl through the breach. I freaked.

"202-553-4223." I pressed Josh's number quickly into the phone.

---

18. A very different trio than the "Lions and Tigers and Bears, oh my!" that had seemed delightful when watching them, from a sanitized distance, on television.

Then I panicked some more.[19] We still had our D.C. area cell phones. I have no idea why. We weren't moving back to D.C. anytime soon, but we couldn't bring ourselves to get rid of the D.C. connection, as if it somehow proved that this Hiawassee Springs idea was just a small stop on the way back to what we had previously known as civilization. The land before unidentifiable animalia in our walls.

"Josh, please please please pick up." I got nothing, just a voicemail. I then, begrudgingly, tried to phone the owners of our guesthouse. Again, voice mail. I left them a message, "Jeannie, this is Lily Walker Stone, with Joshua Stone, um, the tenants from next door. There is some kind of small animal clawing its way into my wall. I'm okay, just a little freaked out. Any idea of what I should do? Please call back if you can. Um, thanks." I hung up from what was the strangest message I had ever left for anyone to date.

At this point I would be negligent if I didn't go into a little more detail about Josh's and my "living situation." You see, Josh and I didn't have a ton of time to plan our arrival in Hiawassee Springs. We met, fell in love, married and moved to the 'wassee faster than some people decide whether to have chicken or fish for dinner. Each of our many decisions (whether to marry, when, where to move, etc.) felt, well, instantaneous. With three weeks before our move to the South, we hadn't yet taken the time to look for a place to live. So accustomed were we to just finding a place quickly in a big city, we hadn't thought it might be difficult.

When we finally had the time, we tried Craigslist. There it was.

"Nice family seeks nice[20] couple to occupy guesthouse for one semester stint. Price is negotiable, people are reasonable."[21]

Josh called right away, and negotiated a rent (sight unseen) that

---

19. This "panic" involved a hoppy little dance around the living room while yelling "Josh, Josh, Josh, where the f**k are you?" as his phone continued to ring without him answering.

20. In retrospect, maybe the usage of "nice" twice within one sentence should have been a tipoff, an indication that the lady doth protest too much. Still, we were dizzy in love. We thought "nice" meant nice.

21. Again, should this have been a clue? If it needs to be said …

was less than a third of what either of us had paid individually to live in D.C. He mentioned that the woman he spoke to, Jeannie Pichee (which she clarified is correctly pronounced "Puh-CHEE" not "Peachy") seemed very nice and convinced him that we would enjoy living in her house. She had two horses, a pony named Macaroni and five dogs. Josh had an upcoming meeting at the University, so he decided to check out our digs and give me the lowdown. Josh, being a man of written words rather than verbal statements, sat down to write me an e-mail about his experience at Jeannie Pichee's compound.

My dear Lilybillygoat,²²
I promised you our life would be an adventure, right? Well here goes. The guest house is adorable, cozy, like a nice writer's cottage. It reminds me of my grandparents' country house in Montreal. There is running water, a big kitchen, and a beautiful view of the great outdoors. It isn't a palace, by any means, but I do think we'll be happy there, at least for one semester, until we have time to find you the home of your dreams … or at least, your Hiawassee Springs dreamhome.
All my love,
Joshycito

My sweet Joshua, always one to woo with words, left out some crucial details about our new abode. I will bullet them for you, the reader, in no particular order of repulsiveness, for your ease and reading pleasure.

Jeannie is married to a large man named Stuart who for some reason is called "Joe C." When said fast it sounds like his name is "Josie," which is a woman's name where I come from. Joe C. is a recovering sex addict who needs structure to maintain emotional equilibrium. To achieve this structured environment, Joe C. enjoys woodworking, which I suppose is another attempt to replace the other work with his hands which got him into trouble with the neighbor's teenage daughter, Mollie Mae. While Joe C. enjoys all kinds of woodwork, he is

22. The author notes, not my real name, but a pet name that Josh likes, and I tolerate, because it makes him happy. Now I understand why my officemate used to pretend to puke into a garbage can every time Josh called me at work.

most fond of right angles. For some reason, they quell those illicit sex cravings like none other. For obvious reasons, I avoid Joe C.

Cockroach fecal matter covers every available surface in the house, especially the kitchen area. At first, I wasn't quite sure what all those black squishy dots were. I asked Jeannie one day, and she said, "Sure as all get go, those here are either mouse or cockroach droppings." I am not entirely sure, but I think I would have preferred a third option.[23]

On three separate occasions[24] I had a cockroach fly into my ear while I was trying to sit and enjoy some quality family programming on the television. You may try to argue with me that "Hey, Lily, cockroaches don't fly." You may be right, I'm not a bug specialist or anything, but I do know this: there is something that looks like a cockroach, has wings and flies and it has flown into an orifice on my head a total of three times. Here, they call these critters "palmetto bugs" and they are the size of a deck of cards. Call them what you will, but they are every bit as unpleasant as they sound.

Love conquers all. Josh and I still managed to find some charm in our "writer's cottage," despite the drawbacks. After we had been living there for four months, and diligently looking for a more permanent – and less infested – place to live, the darnedest thing happened. There was this scratching....

I was sitting on the couch one day, taking in a little *Gilmore Girls*, when all of a sudden I heard a scratching sound. You heard that part. Well, after I called Josh and Jeannie and didn't get an answer, I started looking around the house for something to defend myself with, should the animal show its dirty paws. I managed to gather together a Frisbee, a metal soup ladle, and a heavy box. Don't ask me what I thought I was going to do with that combination, but I reentered the

---

23. Like footprints from tiny little angels that frequent rural Hiawassee Springs neighborhoods late at night, when all the boys and girls of the town are tucked into their happy little beds. Something like that would have been great. Apparently I was asking for too much.

24. Which, for the record, is just frequent enough to ensure that it isn't an entirely random occurrence.

living room ready for combat. Just then, battle regalia in hand, Jeannie and Joe C.'s two young boys pounced through my front door, blabbering about their mom having sent them over, and scrambling over themselves to be the first to see the beast-in-the-wall.

"Sit quietly," I told them in my most convincing stern voice, "I promise you will hear something scratchy very soon."

They complied, and all of fifteen seconds later they heard their first, "Scratch. Scratch Scratch."

They jumped and squealed like the 10-year-old boys they were. Peter and Yoshi[25] were not twins, although they were both born in November, ten years previously. Yoshi Pichee is the Pichees' biological son that they raised from birth. Peter Pichee was Yoshi's best friend from pre-kindergarten and he had lost both his parents in a tragic car accident when he was four years old. Peter was an only child at the time and the court agreed to let him live with the Pichees'. The boys, though biologically not from the same genetic material, might as well have been cloned at birth for how well they got on together. The Pichees' had four kids in addition to Yoshi and Peter, but only the "twins" and an older – and unfortunately strange – seventeen-year old son named Deacon still lived at home.

"I hear it, I hear it!" Peter and Yoshi screamed in delight, in unison, the same way they made their way through life.

At that point, Deacon entered, looking bored, per usual. He had clearly been sent by the parents to check in on their city-girl guest house tenant.

"Yeah, great, guys, you hear the animal." Deacon remained unimpressed.

"Miss Lily, do you think we should scream real loud to make it come out of the wall?" Peter asked. Or it might have been Yoshi who inquired. They really sounded alike. Either way, not important.

At that moment, Joe C. entered the room, his corpulent mid-section

---

25. Yoshi was named for a yogic master that the Pichees met during their 2 year stint in Asia. This time, not coincidentally, overlapped with the period of time when Joe C. was being questioned for some of his less discreet sexual escapades in our precious small town.

flopping and exposed, fresh from a "jog," or playing with the horses. It wasn't entirely clear from the smell. I venture that Joe C. might have been jogging, because he was shirtless, shellacked with sweat, his largeness packed like a sausage into very tiny black shorts, with the requisite long white socks and sneakers.[26]

"Let's see what we have goin' on here," Joe C. bellowed as he sauntered into the room and leaked puddles of perspiration en route to the origin of the scratching. Joe C. then proceeded to get down on one sweaty knee, peer down into the hole that the mystery animal had gnawed into the wall, and noticed some fecal matter below the opening. He then pinched a sizable amount of feces between his thumb and index finger, rolled it around scientifically[27] to check its consistency, and declared, "Yes sirree, this here definitely came from a rodent."

Wow, is all I can say. Mystery solved. What?

Not a moment passed before Jeannie Pichee came in, carrying an unopened box of moth balls. She did so with such nonchalance that it seemed as if everyone keeps a ready box of moth balls next to the sugar bowl just in case such a situation should arise.

"This should do it, Miss Lily. Where is your masking tape?" Jeanie asked as she simultaneously poked around the house. I hated to tell her that since we had opened all our boxes in Hiawassee Springs and not repackaged any, we were fresh out of both moth balls and masking tape. How in the world did we survive?

Jeannie sent Yoshi back to their house, he returned with the masking tape, and we began plugging the hole, but only after we shoved it full of enough moth balls to make it smell like sixteen of your grandmother's old winter coat closets.

"Isn't this cruel?" I asked, wondering about the poor little varmint holed up in the wall. Jeannie wasn't the slightest bit concerned.

"Miss Lily, I saw the proudest lookin' mama squirrel on your porch the other day, and I just know she is using that there wall to make her babies. I have seen her come in and out, so I know she has another

---

26. In a word: hot. I want to believe that in that outfit, in that sweaty state, he could only have been jogging. Work with me.

27. I am not sure what kind of "science" this would be.

exit. This blockade here will just keep her from using your living room for an exit. Sound good?"

I wasn't exactly sure what would possibly sound good about the idea of rodents birthing and rearing in my wall, but from somewhere deep inside, the animal lover in me replied, "Sounds good, Jeannie, just glad they have a way back out."

Chapter 10

Rosa

Querida Diary,

Where was I? Oh right, Ana and me had just arrived and seen the Cuencas at the airport. Señora Cuenca came over to Ana and I and greeted us traditionally, one kiss on each of our right cheeks. She introduced us to Señora Cuenca, and said we would meet her teenage son Martin back at the house that night. Ana and I continued to hold hands, squeezing each other excitedly, but still trying to play it cool as we dragged our heavy bags, and followed the Cuencas toward their car. I remember looking around the parking lot, and my eyes rested on a shiny, black Mercedes I just knew must be the Cuencas' car. Instead, they directed us to a car that probably used to be red, but most of the paint had peeled off. It looked old, it was hot in the car, and with the windows down, we couldn't hear much, so Ana and I just sat through the 15 minute ride back to the Cuenca's house in excited silence, buzzing with what might be.

We got to the house, and the Cuencas immediately showed Ana and me where we would sleep. They had put two sleeping bags on the carpeted floor in the room next to the laundry room. It wasn't grand, but we were too excited to notice. They told us to shower and gave us uniforms to wear, and we changed and headed to the restaurant. We arrived at the restaurant and learned that we would work in the kitchen, cleaning and cutting vegetables and meats, and then, when we got really good at those tasks, and learned more English, we would

be able to work with the customers out front. It was all too much to
take in, especially after our very long trip.

We worked for a few hours, and then headed back to the house
with Martin. He is 17, he took sharp turns with the not-red car,
smoked a cigarette out the window, and well, he is really good looking. Ana and I exchanged glances, saying with our eyes that we had
both noticed how cute our new "cousin" was. He didn't seem to notice
we existed in the back seat, other than when he argued with the
other drivers and yelled bad words at them, he gestured towards the
back seat to look for our agreement. We didn't understand much of
why he was so angry at the other drivers, but we quickly nodded in
agreement with whatever he said.

We went back to our rooms and fell into a deep sleep. The following
morning we were woken up at 5 a.m., to help clean the house and to
help make breakfast for Martin and Señora Cuenca before we all went
to the restaurant. Ana and I worked all day, only stopping for some
toasted bread around 3 p.m., and then back to work. The other workers kept to themselves, and we passed most of the day in silence. The
days continued like that, and after a few days I asked Señora Cuenca
when we were going to go to school and register for classes. She looked
surprised at my question, told me that I had a lot of nerve asking her
such a question, after all that she had done for us. She told me that I
can't go to school right now because it cost so much to bring me from
Jujuy to Miami, and that I need to work to pay it off. There is so
much to pay for: our bus tickets, our plane tickets, our passports, our
food, our place to stay in the house, the gas Martin uses to take us
back from work. Everything is so expensive in America. She listed it
all for me, and it's a lot of money that the Cuencas have laid out to
make this experience happen for Ana and me. I don't want to seem
ungrateful, but I didn't have any idea that it would cost so much

money, that it would take such a long time to earn, or that I would need to pay it back before I could start school again.

And so, the days continued like that, each day the same as the next, except Sundays, when we were permitted to go to Church, and thankfully there was a mass in Spanish, so we could understand the words and sing along to the hymns. One night, during the usual life-threatening rides home with Martin, he started to speak to us. Well, he started to speak to Ana, really. He asked her if she had a boyfriend. She smiled, averted his eyes, and sweetly and sincerely told him no. She had never had a boyfriend. Neither of us had. We were not those kinds of girls. Ana already turned 14, but I am still 13 and not permitted to have boyfriends.

Bye for now,

Rosa

Some things are too personal even for the Diary, some things I don't want other people to know. It's too hard. I'm so embarrassed that I was really jealous at first. I even remember a few nights when I woke up and saw that Ana wasn't sleeping next to me. I looked at the clock on the wall and waited 10 minutes for her to come back from the bathroom. When she didn't come back, I explored the house to find her. I didn't want to wake the Cuencas, so I tiptoed as quietly as possible. After checking a few doors, I entered Martin's room. He had Ana in his bed, and they were moving around under the covers, and I heard her whimper. She sounded like the stray dogs in our old neighborhood, when the mean little boys would corner them and pelt them with rocks. She didn't sound happy. I called her name, and she told me to go away, she said it calmly, but finished with more whimpering.

I waited up for her, and heard her when she crawled into bed. Our sleeping bags were pressed next to each other, but I put mine closer to the wall. She had already made such a large space between us, putting Martin in the middle. I felt betrayed.

I can see now why that was silly, but I didn't understand then. I didn't know that she didn't want to be with him. I only started to figure it out later that night, early in the morning, actually, when Ana went to take a shower, and Martin came to my bed, took out his switchblade, and held it tight against my neck.

"One word about Ana, you stupid little bitch, and I will slit your throat." He pulled so hard on my long, jet-black hair that a few strands came loose and a little blood appeared at the scalp, and then he let go with one last tug, and I curled into a ball, too stunned to cry, too scared to move.

I was too scared to even talk to Ana about it. I didn't know what to do. I spent the next few days in a daze, going through the motions of work and sleep without feeling truly awake. I had thought that Ana was a virgin, like me. We were only thirteen and fourteen, and we had been told to save ourselves for marriage. It is a sin to have sex before marriage and Ana was not a sinner. She was a good girl from Jujuy, like me. I couldn't believe what she was doing with Martin. Sure, he was handsome, but he seemed dangerous, and I thought she wasn't that kind of girl.

Ana never told me about everything that happened with Martin, and we spoke less and less every day. Several months passed; I lost track. I wondered if maybe she blamed me for helping her win the contest that brought her to the United States. It didn't seem like such a great prize now.

I woke up when she left our room every night for Martin, and on the nights that she did not leave herself, he came to get her, roughly grabbing her by the arm, and dragging her with him. I would wake up when Ana came back in, too, and she would walk a little bent over, and crumble into bed. I knew something was wrong, but I was scared to talk to her about anything anymore. I felt so lonely in that house, and the loneliness sat there like a sneaky cat in the room at night, when Ana wasn't there to be my friend and confidant any more.

A few months later, Ana vomited while we were making breakfast. I told her that if she were sick, maybe she could go back to bed and wouldn't have to work. She asked *Señora* Cuenca when she got up, but *la Señora* refused. She told us that we weren't paid to be sick, we were paid to work. Ana asked her, "Are we getting paid?" I remember that moment perfectly, painfully. *Señora* Cuenca slapped Ana in the mouth, and told her that we are costing her a good bit of money, that we had already, and that we are paid every day as we work off our debt. *Señora* Cuenca said that we would see the money in time, but that every day with our eating lots of food, and using the electricity and the shower, we were costing her more money.

One night, when we were getting ready for bed, I saw Ana's naked body as she slipped into her nightgown. She was always thin, and her arms and legs were thinner than ever. Her belly, on the other hand, had a noticeable convex shape, curving outward like she had swallowed a pumpkin. How I missed those pumpkin empanadas, straight from the oven, so much tastier than the fried ones that Maria preferred. Her stomach looked just like one of those delicious treats, and I almost went to her then. She was pregnant, I had no idea how far along, but definitely, unmistakably with child. She saw me looking then, and immediately turned away.

"Ana," I said, unable to form the words to say anything more.

"Don't, Rosa, you'll just make it worse." She spoke to the floor when she did speak, always this way now. I hadn't heard her laugh in longer than I could remember.

We laid down in silence, snuggled in our sleeping bags, palms touching each other, and we both wept quietly. I cried for many reasons. I cried because I was lonely, I missed *Mami* and even Maria. I missed school and our friends and my home and everything. Touching her hand I realized how much I had been missing Ana.

The door opened a crack and we sped apart, knowing it was Martin and not wanting him to see us interact. She groaned to her feet and I heard her steps on the floor as she walked toward his room. Just like that, she was gone.

I fell asleep and at some point I remembered hearing a muffled scream, but I could have been dreaming. I was having a bad dream about two boys in Jujuy that brought guns to a primary school and were holding all the children hostage. Later, I remember hearing Ana stumble into the room, get in her sleeping bag, and go to sleep.

At 5 a.m. that morning, just like every other morning, I woke up to our alarm. Ana didn't get up. She was harder and harder to wake every morning. I wasn't sure if it was because she was pregnant, or because she spent half the night awake in Martin's bed, but she had a much harder time waking up for work than I did.

I called her name. I nudged her. I coaxed her into the day. That didn't work. I knelt down next to her and squeezed her hand. It was cold.

Chapter 11

Mila

Atlanta. It sounded exotic. Atlanta. I think the name sounded so exciting because it reminded me of "Atlantis." I actually did picture it next to the sea, which I knew wasn't true, just from a quick glance at a map. Still, I liked imagining that it was more Atlantis, and less like a sprawling city.

My mom always said that I have a great imagination. I think it's going to help me in my acting career. I will probably only have to work for a few months to have enough money saved to get me to New York City, where things will finally happen for me. I feel like I've been waiting, waiting, waiting for my life to start. My mother always tells me that I am impatient. Of course I am impatient. Look where all that patience got her: spending her whole life in Slovakia, working in that stupid restaurant. It's not for me. I know how to work hard, and I will do it.

I just finished my first week of work. It's not as bad as it could have been for someone who didn't already know their way around a restaurant. I had a few days to settle in and meet some of the other workers in the restaurant before I started in. It's a little like the United Nations here, without the translators. There are about 25 of us living above the restaurant. It's cramped, to say the least. I share a room with 5 other women, 3 of whom speak Spanish, so I guess they could be from Spain or wherever, but I don't really know for sure. There is one girl in the room from the Ukraine, she said, and she seems about my age, but again, we don't speak the same language, so all we can really do is just smile at each other. Still, somehow, I feel like she and I might become friends. Just the same, I am grateful to have a place to live. It's actually really expensive to live in Atlanta, even when I am sharing a room with five other girls. I don't know exactly how much it costs, but Chico says he will just add the cost of the rent to the amount I already owe him for my visa and travel to Atlanta.

Chico is the owner of the restaurant where we work. Well, he co-owns it with his brother, Jose, but it seems like Chico calls the shots. Chico is definitely the more charming of the two. He has dark hair that he wears a little long on top and slicked back, kind of like Al Pacino in Scent of a Woman, but just the hair I mean, because Chico doesn't have trouble seeing. He has tanned muscled arms that he usually shows off in tight fitting white T-shirts, with a tattoo of some kind of Asian symbol on his arm that makes him look tough and sexy. He likes to wear black pants and shiny shoes and carries himself like he is always heading somewhere important and potentially dangerous. He reminds me of a Latin James Dean. He is gruff speaking, but not with me. He has been nothing but gentle to me since we met.

The restaurant where we all work is called "Hunan Palace," but the only Chinese people involved with the whole business are the nine waitresses and one chef. Most everyone else is Hispanic or Spanish speaking, save for Katarina (the Ukrainian girl) and me. We are learning more Spanish than English, which suits me fine, because my English is already very good, so now I am on my way to being trilingual.

The work at the restaurant is somewhat familiar, probably because I am already accustomed to hard work at a restaurant. It is definitely harder to get through the 18 hour shifts without my mom, and harder to do all the work behind the scenes, instead of waiting tables. I never realized how much I liked the attention from all the tourist boys, even though they drove me crazy, it gave me a chance to act. Here at Hunan I spent the last week totally behind the scenes, cutting and peeling fruits and vegetables, dealing with raw meat, which is well, really gross. I don't want to complain, though, because I chose this work, I chose this change, and at worst, it will be six months of work before I head back to mom and maybe to Marek. Poor Marek. I am sure I will have forgotten about him before these six months go by.

There are two bathrooms for the 25 of us in the apartment, which is not great. I can make do for now, but I do wonder what will happen when my time of the month comes around. I just hope that none of us gets sick and has to occupy the bathroom. There could be a riot. Not really, I guess. Everyone seems to get along really nicely. Still, I would be lying if I said that I didn't miss my mother, because I do. I miss working alongside her, each of us carrying dumplings, calling in orders, spinning around each other balancing large trays of hot food. We were a great team, especially as I got older, and she treated me more like a friend, a confidant. In a couple of days I will try to get enough money for a calling card so that I can hear her voice and reassure her that I am okay. I had to break down finally and tell her where I was. That morning, before I left to catch the train, I told her the truth. Sort of. I told her that I was going to America to try my hand at acting.

"But Mila, how will you live if they don't hire you?" She worried out loud. She held my hands in hers, and we sat down together on the worn green comforter, shabbily covering the double bed we shared.

"Mother, do not worry. Haven't you always told me just how pretty I am, with my long blonde hair and sparkling green eyes?" I batted my eyelashes flirtatiously at her, and flipped my straight hair, shiny and thick, always the envy of my classmates, and the joy of the dumpling-eating tourists. That move usually did the trick. It didn't, that time, though, my mother's chin quivered convulsively, while she tapped her left foot like she had shaky leg syndrome. That combination always meant one thing: uncontrollable emotion was afoot.

She didn't cry, although I could tell that she was on the verge, and if the waterworks started, there would be no end. Instead, my mother pulled herself together quickly, as if she knew that when she cries, I tend to shut off. It's a terrible thing to watch a parent cry, and for some reason, my childish response has always been to harden my heart against the pain, count to ten, and to think of acting out the role of spoiled kids I've seen in movies and the ways they treat their American parents.

"Mila, my love, I am serious. How will you survive on your good looks alone? I know that you are smart. Please don't go. You will stay. You will go to University. We will find a way to pay for your tuition, we will find a way to something better. I have tried for you. I have tried and tried and tried and please don't go. Please, my sweet Mila, please don't go." I guess she couldn't help herself. She started to sob, and that quickly turned into yelling and begging and, well, none of it did any good. I mean, I thought about it for a second. Her cries and pleadings definitely tore at my heart, but I didn't let it show. I kept the emotion and the indecision inside for the benefit of both of us. I didn't want her to think that I could be convinced that maybe it wasn't a good idea to go to the U.S. I am eighteen years old, already. It is time for me to find my own way, do my own thing, get out and see the world. It would have been so much easier to stay in Bratislava, but also harder in a way. I would have spent every day wondering what if, and I don't want to live my life that way.

"Mom, you have always told me that I can make you laugh, that I am a natural born actress. You didn't bring me into this world to shut me into a little box and let me suffocate. I am a beautiful bird with big wings that need to stretch, or I'll just die here. In my little box. I'll die." I raised a dramatic hand to my head and tried my best southern accent from America that I had seen in *Steel Magnolias*, this movie from the 1980s. It worked, she finally laughed. Still, it was an uneasy laughter, and I doubt she was truly convinced.

Chapter 12

Lily

After six months of work, I am about to be unemployed. Rumor has it that our funding is about to be cut. Six months of building relationships with clients. Clients who depend on me to help them feel safe and have legal status in the U.S. Maybe I'm delusional, but I really feel like my clients need me. I am the only provider of free immigration legal services in Hiawassee Springs.

What if I work for free instead? My mom already thinks I just about do. Maybe I could give up my salary entirely and represent clients without getting paid and then just waitress on the side? I mean, coming from D.C., the cost of living in Hiawassee Springs is only a fraction of my former expenses. That said, I used to work at a private law firm, so I had more money to spend. Josh and I have been talking it over for weeks. We almost always have the same conversation, with few variations.

"Lily, I want you to be happy."

"But I am happy, Joshycito, I love you."

"I am not egotistical enough to believe that loving me is enough, Lily. I know you miss your friends, your family, and the life you used to have in D.C. before I dragged you here." He pouted.

Hearing him recognize what I "gave up" to be with him filled my heart with love. I just wanted to squeeze him and never let go.

"Lily, I think this job makes you happy. Do you want to stay at the IJC and just work without pay for awhile? The funding may come back, right?"

My Josh, always the optimist.

"Lovey, the funding is not coming back."

"But it could, right? Or you could canvass the community doing fundraising? Or you could contact your old firm or the national lawyer organizations and see if they want to help fund legal services for immigrants?" Josh lit up with each new idea, as if he had just invented a solution to global warming. He truly believed that he could fix anything that ailed me.

"Sweetie, I will try all of those ideas. They are really good suggestions, and I will give it a shot." I didn't think they were good suggestions at all, but I didn't have the heart to tell him he didn't know the slightest thing about my line of work.

One month later, the conversation basically repeated, with a new infusion of sound, reasonable suggestions from Josh. I'll save you the repetition and start basically where we left off a month earlier.

"Lily, I want you to be happy and, if there are no other funding options, I think you should keep working there pro bono."

"Um, earth to Josh, I am already barely getting paid, and nice try to use the legalese, but I am already doing pro bono work with my public interest job. Now I will actually be a volunteer instead of a hired employee. Any other bright ideas?"

Okay, I got testy. I know I just told you that I, too, thought about working for free. For some reason it bothered me only when Josh suggested it, and not when I thought it up myself. I get far more moody than Josh does. Somehow, this angel of a man manages never to get mean or rude or make ad hominem attacks. He always means what he says, and especially when it comes to me, he always means well. It's infuriating.

"Lily, I just think—"

"Joshua," I interrupted, (and he never gets mad when I interrupt), "I will follow through with my current clients as far as I can, but I won't take on any new ones. The IJC can pay my salary for the next two months, and then I will start looking for another job."

He looked sad. Joshua the poet, the English professor, is a contemplative soul. He feels tension more sensitively and acutely than the rest of the population. He furrowed his brow and nudged around a few magazines that he had left strewn across the dusty pine floors with his naked foot.

"I'm afraid, Lily, that if you don't like your job you'll start feeling unhappy here and then you'll be unhappy with me. I can't lose you. You are my everything." He choked a bit on the last few words, and then became very quiet, and looked down at the floor.

I can't really promise not to be unhappy. I wanted to, but I didn't, because, I mean, you can say the words, you can even really mean them when they come out of your face, but it's an impossible promise to keep. I knew that I would be disappointed to leave the IJC, after only six months of work and with so much left undone. I made a promise to myself to do the best that I could do for my clients, and then to work hard to find another job that I would really enjoy. I think Josh knew that I was just trying to make do with an unfortunate situation. He offered another well-meaning suggestion.

"Lily," he had composed himself to a less sad Josh by now, "maybe this IJC thing might be a blessing in disguise. Maybe now would be a good time to try to start our family."

Like an explosion inside me, I felt every emotion at once, and shards of my former, pre-married self lodged into my heart, my brain, and my gut. I didn't even know what to say. I am thirty-five years old, I am married to the man I want to spend forever and after with, and I have already finished all the schooling I ever want to do. Why was I freaking out about this?

"Josh, I'm not sure that I'm ready."

His face fell. He made a motion with his mouth like he wanted to say something, and then he stopped. He just got quiet. He picked up a copy of the New York Times. I could see from the date on the top that it was the one from last Thursday, and I knew that he had read every article already. I think he just wanted to bury himself in something for a while, and he can lose himself easily in the written word. It's his best medium.

"Joshua." I barely knew what to say to make it okay. I tried, "I really love you." At that moment, I tried to convey everything with those words. I wanted him to know, to feel, that I loved him, wanted him, needed him, but I could tell that nothing I could say other than, "yes, let's have children," would have been enough.

I racked my brain and my heart to figure out why I was having this reaction. My parents had been telling me for years that after age thirty, I would be a higher risk pregnancy, especially given our family history. They had already mentioned, not with great subtlety and more than a few times, that I should be ready to have a baby, especially now that I was married. I love kids, I really do. My sister already has three of them, and I am head over heels crazy for them.

James, Ella and Ruby. They are healthy and rambunctious and so much fun. I love watching the way my parents adore grandparent-dom, and cherish the birthday parties, and the special "booberry" pancakes that my little niece Ella loves for my mom to make. I love my parents enough to want to give them more little joyful people to appreciate them, and I want to give Josh a baby if he wants one, it's just … I am not done yet.

Something inside me has changed. It is not just the move from our bustling nation's capital, to this sleepy, seductive town. It is the people. It is the work. It has become not just something that I do, but something that I am. I am now a public interest lawyer, a human rights attorney. My work has become inextricably intertwined with my identity, and I don't want to have to learn to be anyone else. I feel the most me I have ever felt, and I know that having a baby would change everything. With a baby, well, the baby has to come first. I know that. I would want for it to be that way. And yet, right now, I want to put my work, my clients, before anything else.

I know that I am part of something at the IJC. I am part of the so-lution. I don't mean to be very dramatic about my work, but it feels important and timely. It feels essential and I can't stop it now. Having my funding yanked at the same time that Josh is starting to ask about kids makes me feel like I am standing on a carpet while the ground is dragged from beneath my feet, leaving me stranded.

It's horrible to say, but having a baby now would be like making a concession. I would feel folded back into my previous self. That self worked at a big law firm, and woke each day to too much caffeine, an overtoasted bagel on my way out the door, fake smiles for my col-leagues, false assurances to my clients in Shanghai and Munich and wherever else I was doing business. Without even meeting my clients, I would leave the office, grab a drink with friends, whine about being single, trudge home to my apartment, and sleep the sleep of the un-concerned. Then I would wake up seven hours later and do it again. Each day, Sunday through Sunday, I lived like the suit that I was. I felt less than whole, but I assumed that what I needed was a great boyfriend, someone with whom to enjoy all the things that I didn't do myself because I assumed that they would be better done with someone else. Who had the time, anyway, for paddle boating in the tidal basin? I put my life on hold waiting for the special guy to come, to take me to the FDR memorial as the sun set, to sniff in those cherry blossoms one week each spring, to leisurely walk around the Mall and the capitol admiring the greenery and the stately buildings. I promised myself that I would be different when I had someone to share it all with, I would stop working, every day, from early in the morning till late at night. I was my work then, too, I suppose, although I was a shell of my current self.

Now, I wake each day to a wonderful man. He slides a protective arm around me when he feels me rise early to do some yoga before work.[28] His breath is warm and a bit smelly and he leans in close and tells me that I am beautiful and loved. I slide out of bed, and after enough stretches to make me feel strong and balanced and ready for the challenge of the day, I take a steaming hot shower,[29] and pad into the kitchen to make us breakfast. I sleep fitfully for most of the night, thinking of my clients, excited for the day, worried about what they will do if our funding is gone, wondering if I should just do it for free.

Having a significant other definitely has given me the freedom to savor life a little more, but I can see now that I was waiting for someone to come and fill a void in my life that I had made myself. My half-Puritan roots and the corresponding work ethic make it so that my work in many ways is my identity. Without my work, I would just be a woman who gave up her high-powered job to live in small-town America with her man. That story is fine for someone else, but it isn't my story. I am Lily Walker Stone. I am now an immigration attorney first, and someone's wife second.

And so, I return to my dilemma. I find myself sad and spent at the end of each work day, more so than usual. I feel like I am running against the hourglass, and each passing day means fewer people that I will be able to help.

---

28. I hear that yoga is relaxing and good for me, so I'm giving it a go. I basically just sit with my legs crossed breathing in and out for as long as I can stand it before collapsing in boredom.

29. This house might be infested with all kinds of animalia, but the shower has never disappointed.

You see, people in most situations are not entitled to lawyers. It's not a right, and it's not an entitlement. If you are in a certain kind of criminal case, you automatically receive a public defender. If not, you can fend for yourself. So, if you are a woman, whose husband met you in Mexico, and brought you to the U.S. to marry you, and you think you are in love and loved in return, and then one day, that man decides that he can treat you as he pleases, and he begins to hit you, hard, all the time, because it has been three years already, and you have not given him a son, and he tells you that if you report the abuse to the police that he will deport you, and your family in Mexico will be ashamed of you, it is a bit overwhelming to say the least. The U.S. Congress has decided that you have the right to petition for your own immigration status, so that this abusive man cannot hold the fact that you are not yet legally here in the U.S. over your head. The only catch is that you need to know about this right, and you really need an attorney to help you through the process. And what if you live near Hiawassee Springs and you spend all day working in the fields? One season it is tomatoes, another oranges, and the days pass slowly. You are exhausted, working outside in the endless heat and humidity without time to catch your breath and to seek legal advice, even though your friend from the fields knows about the IJC and knows that there is an Attorney Lily to help you with your immigration papers. It's not like you can afford to have your own car, and your husband picks you up and drops you off at work, and between work and his abusive "love" and the house you must keep tidy to avoid another beating, there just isn't time to think past today. It is hard enough for this woman to find a way to my office, so that together we can end the cycle of abuse, and she can make a fresh start for herself in the U.S. Who will she turn to when I am no longer here?

I can't quit, I just can't do it. The needs of this migrant community are too large, and too invisible. I don't want to work for free, either. I will just have to find a way to stay connected to this commitment I feel to my clients and their needs. I will find a way because I have the education and the means to do it. I will find a way first and foremost, and starting a family will have to wait until I am finished. Whenever that may be.

Chapter 13

Rosa

Miami, Florida
September 22, 2005

Querida Diary,

I have been scared to write for a while, because I don't want Martin or the Cuencas to find my Diary and beat me again. I know now that they are capable of bad things and I am scared. I am scared every day. Still, if I don't write, they will have taken every last thing from me, and then, I don't think that I could go on living anymore.

It has been a little more than three months since Ana died. When I woke, and she was gone, I didn't know if I would be able to get up. I saw dark red blood spilled into a lopsided oval stain underneath Ana. What had Martin done to her? Did he try to get rid of the baby? I held her cold body, felt the bulge in her abdomen, and said goodbye to Ana, and to the baby that she would never have. Something inside me died that day along with Ana. I laid there with her, sobbing, wanting to die along with her when Señora Cuenca bolted in.

"Get up, you lazy girls," I remember her yelling at us. She shook Ana violently, as if to wake her from death. Even *Señora* Cuenca, who I no longer think so highly of, gasped in horror when she saw Ana's exposed stomach and felt for her departed pulse, realizing that Ana was not only pregnant, but also dead.

"Jorge!!" she called, "*Ven aqui. Ahora!*" Come here now, she said to *Señor* Cuenca. He came into the room, his mouth gaped open in shock, and then looked to me.

"This is not a holiday, Rosa. Get dressed, and start making the coffee for Martin. He will take you to work today."

"But what about Ana?" I glanced down toward Ana's body, lifeless on the stained rust-colored carpet. I didn't want to leave Ana with the Cuencas. I didn't know what they would do with her. I didn't trust them anymore.

Señora Cuenca responded by hitting me in the face, turning me around, and kicking me in my backside. "Get out of here now," she growled, "or you will make me very sorry that we opened our home to you two *indias*."

I went, insulted, scared, and dreading the car ride alone with Martin. I tarried over my tasks as long as reasonably possible. Not only did I think Martin was disgusting for the things he had done to Ana, but he was genuinely dangerous. I didn't want him near me.

"Let's go, *fea*," Martin said, as he called me "ugly" and turned me about the shoulder, dragging me towards the car to leave for work. The drive to work was only a few minutes, but it felt like hours. As soon as we were alone in the car, he thrust his hand into my private area, and he spit these words at me.

"*Fea*, we own you now. You will do as I say or what happened to your little whore friend will happen to you, too. You say one word about Ana, to anyone, and I will fuck you and kill you tonight and leave you for dead."

We parked, and I got out of the car with Martin, and went into the restaurant for work. I felt numb. I felt scared. I felt like Jujuy was another life, like another universe I used to be a part of. I felt dead, and I felt ashamed that Martin had touched me. I stumbled through that day, accidently slicing into the side of my hand when cutting vegetables. It hurt, and it bled a lot, but I didn't seek help or pity, because I knew none was coming.

At the end of the day, Martin drove me home, and he said more bad things about Ana. He tried to make it sound like she deserved to be dead. I tried my best to tune him out. Instead, I imagined what Mami and Maria and I would be doing at 9 p.m. on any random Thursday. I thought about the three of us, doing chores at home, making our home clean and nice. The images got me through the car ride home, and lasted until I walked into our room and saw that Ana's sleeping bag was gone. It was just me now.

Diary, I still don't know where the Cuencas took Ana's body. In our culture, it is sacrilegious to bury someone without ceremony. Their soul will live in endless turmoil. I worry about Ana and her soul. I am angry now. I never used to be an angry person, even when Papi died. I was sad then, but now I am sad and angry, and I may get to a point where I cannot take this anymore, and I'll just explode into a million pieces, scattering myself across the Cuencas' carpet like shattered glass.

I feel like I need to tell someone what has been happening here, happening to me, or I will die myself. I am desperately frightened, and I write to you, so that there will be a record of me, so that people besides Mami and Maria will know that I was a girl who came to America, and that I existed, and that I had a friend named Ana and that she is gone. I need them to know that I am completely alone now.

Señora Cuenca let me call Mami last week. We had planned for me to call on that day before I left Jujuy. Mami waited by the phone in our village for three hours to make sure that she didn't miss my call. She sounded so very happy to hear my voice and to know that I was okay. Señora Cuenca stood over me the entire time and threatened me before the call that if I said anything bad about them she would kill Mami and Maria, so that I knew what I could not say. It is better anyway that Mami not know how they are making me live. She would feel very sad if she knew and I don't want Mami to be sad, especially not because of me.

She was sad enough about Ana. Ana's parents had died when she was a little girl, and she was being raised by her grandparents. They were religious people, believing in spirits and the devil and all that, as well as in Jesus Christ after the missionaries came. Señora Cuenca had lied to Ana's grandparents and told them that Ana was in a very bad car accident, and that she had wrecked their car and hadn't pulled through, even though Señora Cuenca stayed at her bedside in the hospital for three days and didn't sleep day or night. I'll give it to Señora Cuenca, she certainly is creative in her cruelty. Anyway, Mami said that Ana's grandparents believe that the same devil that took their daughter away came and took her granddaughter Ana, and that they are very unlucky people. Señora Cuenca told them that Ana's hospital bills were very high and so Ana's grandparents are now trying to send the Cuencas money to pay for Ana's debt. I want to tell them that the Cuencas are murderers and liars, but I am left to scream inside my head. Maybe one day others will know, but not today.

For the next few weeks after Ana died I thought many times about approaching the Cuencas about when I would be starting school. You may have thought that after Ana died and her body disappeared, that I would have buried my dreams along with her. I didn't. I wanted so much to believe that my going to school was not a lie like everything else. I remember the last time that I tried to ask the Cuencas about school. It was a Sunday, and we were about to head to church, and I was feeling hopeful that maybe the Cuencas would make good on their promise. I could hear all the Cuencas in the showers as I tried to clean up the best that I could for misa, the Sunday mass.

Sunday had easily become my favorite day of the week, the only day that showed any distinction between one day and the next. I would wake at 5 a.m., and begin to clean the house, as quietly as I could, so as not to upset or anger the Cuencas. At around 9 or 10 they would wake, enter the kitchen, and demand breakfast, which I would make, serve and clean up until around noon. They would then begin to shower and get ready for misa.

The house has two showers: one in Señor and Señora Cuenca's bathroom, and one in Martin's. In the first week or so, I took a shower in Martin's shower whenever I had the chance, whenever he wasn't busy looking at himself for hours in the bathroom. Now, things are different. I am only permitted to use the shower twice a week, and the Cuencas say that my 15 minute shower was costing them too much money, so they shut off the hot water before I go to take my shower. I can only bear a few minutes in the chilly water before I need to come out.

I miss the days of showering in Jujuy. During the summers, we showered right as the sun would set, so that the warmth of the day would be at its peak, and there was always about 10 minutes of warm delicious water before the cool night set in.

Lately, Señora Cuenca always finds something wrong with whatever I am doing. Either there is a spot on the mirror that I cleaned, or the floor has some dust, or the covers on the beds should be tucked more tightly into the edges. I try my best to please them, but I am always wrong. They find ways to punish me. They forbid me from showering and tell me that I am ugly, and an animal, and that I should shower in the backyard like my people like to do.

I once tried to tell them, as nicely as I could – even though the anger rose up inside me, and gripped a tight fist around my heart – my people did not shower out in plain view without any clothes on, but Señora Cuenca hit me in the face so hard that my cheek was swollen and purple for a week. I bit back the pain and didn't cry. I didn't want to give her the satisfaction. I thought, instead, about Ana. Sometimes I see her face when things get really hard here. I think of her, and I see her looking like the Ana I knew before, always with a joke and a smile. Sometimes I see her looking like she did at the end: sad and defeated. I see her here, all the time.

Anyway, we were getting ready to go to church. I was dressed and dusting the living room, and Martin was still in his shower, and

Señora Cuenca in hers. Señor Cuenca emerged, looking clean and well mannered and ready to kneel before God. I thought it might be the perfect time to talk to him about my starting school here. I walked over to him as he sat, on the worn, faded, brown sofa and flipped the channels on the large color television. I began, head cowed, and meekly asked, "Um, Señor Cuenca?"

"What now?" He responded, distractedly, without even turning his head from the variety show on Telemundo. He laughed at the fat man and the skinny woman telling jokes on the screen.

I mustered my courage and began, "I would very much like to go to school here. I was a good student in Argentina and I would like to continue my studies and be a writer or a teach—"

He cut me off, and without taking his eyes off the screen, grabbed me by my hair and pulled my head down into his lap.

He spat into my face, "Sucia, you and your dirty, little friend have cost us more money and caused more trouble than you can imagine. You will stay and you will work, and that will teach you more than school could. You will do as I say, and that is the end of this school nonsense."

And it was.

Goodbye Diary,

Rosa

Chapter 14

Mila

Life at the restaurant in Atlanta is different than my life was at the restaurant in Bratislava, but some of the change is good. I have fallen in love. It's Chico. He makes me feel like a real woman. Marek, poor Marek, is a thing of the past now, just like I knew he would be. Each night after work, instead of cramming into that dreadful overpacked apartment above Hunan with all the other workers, (which I can admit now was a pretty awful apartment, even though I was trying to be upbeat and positive about the situation), I go home with Chico. He is nice to me, gives me chocolates and dinner, and we sleep together and it's good. The only bad thing about the situation is that Jose, his brother, is a big idiot. I wish Chico and I could have the place to ourselves. I pretend to like Jose, but it's not an easy acting job, even for someone as talented as me.

One morning, after I spent the night in Chico's bed, Chico left extra early in the morning to receive a shipment of pork products from the warehouse. While I was sleeping, Jose crawled into his brother's bed with me, pinned me down, and tried to make me have sex with him. I refused, of course.

"Come on, Mila, I know you want me," he breathed into my ear with his foul smelling idiot breath.

"I don't," I said, and meant it, "now get off me or I'll tell Chico."

He laughed at me, and pinned my arms harder against the bed while he used his knees to spread open my legs. I was sleeping in nothing but one of Chico's t-shirts and I felt vulnerable and scared. "Oh, you'll tell Chico, eh? Who is he going to believe, *nena*? His brother, his blood and family, or some *puta* he's been screwing for the last few months?"

I struggled to free an arm and poked Jose in the right eye, squirmed out from underneath him, grabbed my underwear, shoes, and a pair of pants, and ran out the door. I kept running, down the stairs, out to the street, until I realized that I was standing outside, it was cold, and I was half-dressed. I could see the faint light of the digital clock of a bank building close by. It was not yet five in the morning. I quickly threw on the clothes I had carried in my hands, but not before I stepped on something sticky, brown, and unidentifiable. I had to get to work in about 30 minutes, and I didn't know the bus route from Chico's house because he had taken me in his car every morning since I started spending the night. Was there even a bus route that went this far out into the city? I certainly didn't have money for a cab. I didn't have a single dollar on me to buy anything. I dreaded the dawning reality that I would need to go back inside and get a ride from Jose.

"Arghhhhhhhhhhhhhhhhhh!!!!!!" I screamed into the night air, Brando-like, harkening back to his "Stella!!!!!"

The street answered me back with its silence, not a soul yet moving at that hour, save for a few stirring people, nestled into alleyways, covered with newspapers, trying to get some sleep. I never would have thought that people in America could be so poor. Eastern Europe, sure, but America? I have seen the movies, but I was never sure what was real and what wasn't, whether the people without homes I saw on the screen were just actors, or extra people, or something true that really happens. I just couldn't conceive that it was possible in this rich country for some to have so much and others nothing at all. I stood, feet in that sticky warm mess, and thought about the poor people in America for as long as I could manage before I turned my head back to the reality waiting for me on the fourth floor.

I felt like I had grown an actual tail that was tucked and hanging between my legs, bruised in the places where Jose had tried to force me to be his. Chico kept promising to make me a key to his place, but he hadn't yet, and I was locked out of the apartment I didn't even want to enter.

"Who is it?" Jose called sarcastically in a sing-song way, as he slid aside the keyhole to peer at my face, distortedly close in the circular view.

"It's me, Jose. It's Mila. Who else would it be at this hour? I have to get to work, don't you? Don't play games, Jose. Please, open up and let's go." I tried my best to sound kind and patient, but it was a real stretch.

"I just see a *puta* out there, and *putas* aren't allowed in this apartment. Go away, *puta.*" He laughed and laughed. I wish I had had any power to bargain with at that point.

"Please, Jose, it's cold out here and I stepped in something and I need to wash off my foot. Please open up. We both need to get to work." I tried to sound nice, but I was getting very angry, having to beg this big jerk to take me back inside. Why did Chico leave me with his Godforsaken idiot brother?

"*Puta*, let me see that you are really sorry and then I will let you back in. Get down on your knees, like I know you like to, and beg me for forgiveness, and then, maybe, I'll consider letting you back inside. After that, maybe, I will think about taking you to work."

Leaving my dignity somewhere outside that door, I did as I was told. I got down on my knees. I told him I was very sorry, would he please accept my forgiveness. I hated doing it, but I knew that if I didn't get to work on time, Chico would be mad, and things were going so well that I didn't want to make him angry. After a few more back and forth exchanges with Jose the idiot jerk, he finally let me in, made me kiss him on the mouth, and called me a *puta* again and again. I cleaned up what was undeniably human waste on my foot, got into my clothes for work, and off we were to Hunan.

We passed most of the ride in silence. I didn't bring up what happened in the apartment, and Jose didn't either. I tried my best to memorize the route to work, but Jose drove too fast, zigzagging between cars like we were filming a chase scene in an action movie. Jose seemed to be creating his own reality, oblivious to the fact that he was driving an old beat up car, even though he put on the fancy tires and the purple neon light blinking from below.

I got out of the car, grateful to be alive, both wired and exhausted from the morning's events, and we filed into work. Jose took a seat in his office in the restaurant, a little side room where they tallied the earnings for the day and drank small cups of strong coffee with lots of sugar. I noticed a calendar filled with naked or mostly naked women over his desk. It was already three years out of date, displayed the wrong month as well, and someone had drawn a moustache on the woman. I wondered what that beautiful blonde woman was thinking when the picture was taken. Was she happy? She was smiling in her tiny bikini, back arched and posed on the shiny red car. Was she just using her beauty to pay the bills while she went to University like her mother wanted her to? I wondered what that woman in the picture is doing now. I wondered if she, too, was trying to get to New York City.

I got down to work, beheading, de-feathering, and cleaning bloody chickens, then chopping their slimy, pale bodies into little boneless bits for the kung pao chicken. Almost nothing is thrown away in the back of Hunan. Whatever we don't use gets made into sauces and soups and served at the weekly buffet on Thursdays. Seeing how the food gets made makes me wary of eating out in a restaurant, or consuming anything that I didn't actually make myself. We, all of the employees, are told that we can't throw anything away, and so we don't. Our customers eat the scraps instead.

I took a place at the cutting table next to Katarina, which she had shortened to the more American "Kat" these days. We had been getting along nicely until I left the room we shared and moved in with Chico. He's really handsome, and I think she is jealous.

"Hi, Kat," I said, over the din of the powerful vacuum, cleaning up the blood and bones from the floor. "How are you doing?"

She shrugged, and made a gesture towards her ears, signaling that she could not hear me over the sounds of the cutting, cleaning and assorted machines. She looked sad to me, and I wondered if she was still mad or jealous because I left, or if she really couldn't hear me. No bother. I had the whole day to myself to dream. I had an especially good plan for that day. I would pretend that I was playing the part of Nicole Kidman portraying a journalist, exploring the restaurant industry. I "acted" out the rest of the day, letting my mind create the script I would recite to the news media that night about the "bloody" life of a restaurant worker.

I was somewhere in between dramatically exiting the restaurant and getting made up for my evening appearance on the most watched news channel in New York City when I caught a glimpse of Chico. He and Jose were in the front office, yelling about something, and I hoped that it had nothing to do with me. They seemed angry with each other, but their relationship was like that at times. The brothers were fiercely close, having come to this country from Colombia with nothing but a little cash and each other. They fought, but knew, not even so deep down, that they really needed each other, and so as hard as they fought, their love ran even deeper.

And so it was. When I glanced back a few minutes later, I caught the brothers giving each other a quick hug. Their fiery tempers had subsided and they no longer seemed angry about anything. Chico's hand lingered on his big brother's smaller shoulder, giving it a squeeze. I remember being surprised when I discovered that Jose was older than Chico. Chico is bigger, stronger, smarter, more capable and seems in charge of everything. I wondered how Jose's ego could stand being the lesser of the two in every way. Maybe that's why Jose was such a jerk.

A little while later Chico and Jose wandered into the back room to check in on the employees. All of us workers had to ask if we could use the bathroom and were allowed two separate five minute breaks during the day. If we took any more time, our pay was docked. I guess. Chico kept track of all of my money for me. It was very hard to have time to eat or use the bathroom, and sometimes days passed when we did neither.

For me, though, things had definitely been more pleasant since I became Chico's girl. Most days, at some point during the day, Chico would take me into the closet where we kept the mop and the cleaning supplies, lock the door, push me up against the wall, and have his way with me. I didn't mind at all. He is a strong Latin man and he has a big sexual appetite. I loved him and wanted to keep him happy with me. Also, he didn't deduct the time we spent in the closet from the other breaks that I was allowed, which was nice, especially when Chico brought me some candy or chocolates into the closet, so it was like I got some food and a "break" and I still had more free time later to use the bathroom.

I noticed, though, that when I came back to work after "closet time" with Chico that the other employees didn't like talking to me. They weren't mean, exactly, but cold. Distant. They started to act like they had never seen me before, like we didn't know each other. Like we didn't work alongside each other every single day. Whatever. Wasting time with them was not going to jumpstart my acting career anytime soon. Besides, it's not like Chico was ever going to spend time in the closet with them. Let's face it, I was way prettier than all of them and I guess they hated me for it.

I caught a glimpse of Chico's muscular torso out of the corner of my eye. His eyes caught mine and he winked; the dimple on his right cheek pronounced and beautiful. He was so hot. I didn't really want to leave him anytime soon. I made a mental note to talk to him later about my visa. I had been in America five months already and I knew that one more month with Chico would not be enough. I needed more time with him. I needed more time to make the kind of money I needed to get to New York, and to send to my mother so that she knew I was doing well. I needed to extend my visa.

The rest of the day and most of the evening passed uneventfully. My body worked hard at the cleaning and cooking, but my head continued in the role of Megan Juvet, the half-Irish, half-French journalist on a journalistic expedition/exposé of the life of a worker in a Chinese restaurant.

At around 10 p.m., Chico opened the door to our workspace and gave me the signal, an upward gesture of the head towards the front door. Chico did not like to be kept waiting. I quickly put down my mop, said goodbye to Kat as if she cared at all, and headed home in the car with Chico and Jose. Jose, jerk that he is, offered me the backseat. As she deftly crawled into the cramped rear space of the car, Journalist Megan Juvet observed: "The age of chivalry, ladies and gentleman, is officially dead."

We drove home and headed upstairs to the apartment. When Chico saw the bed, he cocked his head to one side and sighed.

"Mila, don't be such a slob, okay? Why didn't you make the bed today? What has gotten into you, *nena*?" He was not the slightest bit pleased, but he seemed to be holding back from anger.

I always make the bed and clean the house. This was the first time since I started staying with the brothers Jimenez that I ever messed up even the slightest bit. I felt terrible, and didn't plan to ever do it again. I didn't know how to respond to Chico. I didn't want him to know about the morning's "interaction" with Jose. I just couldn't tell Chico about Jose, what he did or tried to do, or any of it. I knew that Jose was right, that blood was thicker than me, even if I gave Chico something that Jose couldn't. Instead, I just swallowed it and lied.

"Oh my love, I am so sorry. What a silly girl I am, I just completely forgot and I was running late, and then, well, it will just never happen again. Please forgive me," I snuck up to him and kissed him flush on the lips, then his ear, then spread soft kisses all over his neck. He was such a big man, and although I'm tall, my head barely came up to his shoulders.

"Okay, Mila, okay," he laughed at my overt and somewhat pathetic attempt to win him over. I lured him back onto the bed and we made love. When it was over, and I knew he was happy with me, I thought it would be a good time to talk to him about my visa.

"Chico, I don't want to go back to Bratislava next month."

"Why would you, my little Mila?"

"Well, Chico, my visa is up next month, and then I have to go. It makes me really sad, because I need to get to New York City still, and my friends will have finished high school and forgotten me, and I haven't even had a chance to pay back all the money I owe or to get out of Atlanta or—"

"Hush, Mila." Chico clamped his hand down over my mouth. "Mila Mila Mila. You don't have to be bothered with such things." With a laugh he said, "Worrying will make you old and I'll have to replace you. I came here as an immigrant, just like you, and I know how this system works. I will take care of everything for you. I am your guy. I take care of you, I protect you, and I will keep you safe here." As he said everything I needed to hear, he wrapped his big strong arms around me and smoothed back my hair.

"Thank you, thank you thank you, Chico." I punctuated each "thank you" with a fiercely loud smack of a kiss. "I don't know what I would do without you."

Chapter 15

Lily

I can hear my heart beating in my ears. It's loud, and my hands feel slippery. Maybe my uncle won't find me here, hiding under the desk in my father's home office. I can still hear laughter and talking above the music coming from the living room. I try to quiet my thumping heart by singing a lullaby to myself, quietly, in my head. I stop my quiet singing. What is that? Thump. Thump. Thump. My ear is pressed close to the ground. I can hear footsteps. Oh God, no. Please let it not be my uncle. "Lilianaaaaa, where are youuuu?" I can hear him calling my name. I try to curl farther into myself, balled up on the ground, huddled under the old oak desk. The footsteps stop. "There you are," he says. "Were you hiding from someone, foolish little girl?" I look into his face, but his eyes are replaced with oozing pools of blood.

I woke up panting and sweaty all over. The uncle bleeding-eye dream. It had been years since I'd seen that face, felt that fear. I'd had enough therapy to know what it meant and to try to get over my childhood traumas from that bastard uncle of mine, but here it was again. I sigh, peel away the covers from my overheated body, and get out of bed.

I feel anxious and exhausted. Time feels like it is running out for me, and more importantly, for my clients. Nothing feels easy these days. I thought moving to Hiawassee Springs was hard, but fighting for the ability to stay in this town in a job that has come to mean so much to me and my clients is a whole other thing.

One of the hardest parts these days is what all of my mood swings are doing to my sweet Joshua. I know that he wants so desperately to be supportive of me, and even though he says that he is, he feels miles away since our discussion about the baby. I was going through our mail last week and I came across a letter from Cornell. Okay, it was addressed to Professor Joshua Stone and not to me, which I understand is a federal offense, but in our sorting of household duties,

74

I am in charge of opening and filing the mail. So, I opened and read the letter, and it was from the head of the English department at Cornell, who was responding to a request Josh had made for information about their hiring needs and tenure clock, and well, Mr. Dean of English seemed very interested in Josh and his "enormous talent." Oh my God. Was Josh looking for a way out of Hiawassee Springs? Was he looking for a way out with me? Or without? I filed the letter for Josh, and put it in a separate filing cabinet in my head, where I'll store it until I figure out what in the world to do with that information.

When not building new defenses against my husband who might secretly be plotting to leave me, I divide my time these days between caring for my clients and trying to find new sources of funding to keep our operation afloat. I have even more trouble sleeping through the night these days, and my dreams are plagued with disturbing images.[30] Without the funding, there won't be any more clients. I haven't yet turned anyone away, but I know that fateful damn day is coming when I will have to learn to say no.

While the sand floods out of the hourglass at the IJC, I have been savoring the time we have left by working with some remarkable peo-

---

30. Oh come on, are you really that curious? Do you really need to know every alarming thought my crazy little head comes up with? If you must, I will indulge you. Well, there was the circus dream, where I was the dancing bear in the tutu, and I was embarrassed by the little pink tutu that I had to wear, and I tried to complain to the head of the circus (who was that green lizard from the car insurance commercial with a Cockney British accent and he just held his little green belly and laughed at me). Then, just two nights ago, I had a dream that Josh and I were living in Greenland (which is the cold and icy one, often confused with Iceland, which is the pretty country with the great view of the Northern Lights, and the beautiful women that pirates used to steal) and I was pregnant with triplets. After they were born, Josh's family moved to Greenland to help us take care of the kids and I couldn't handle it, so I skipped town with a local pilot, and we moved to the part of Alaska where we spent half the year bathed in light, and half the year shrouded in darkness, and all year long with a pet Moose named "Sphinx." I loved that moose, and I liked the pilot well enough, but still, I missed Josh and the kids, growing up in Greenland without me.

ple. Just a few weeks ago, I had a pair of sisters enter my office. I knew
we'd be friends for life when these two little ladies asked if I was the
same age as them — Angelique and Meronelle are 15 and 17. I, as
you know, am not. They feigned shock that I was, as they said, "so
old." I liked them just a tiny bit less after that comment, but really,
just a tiny bit. Their story seemed remarkable to me when they told
it, although remarkable is a concept that loses its impact when you
see, again and again, the ways that people hurt, abuse and exploit
each other, especially the ones that they love.

"Angie" and "Meronie" were 8 and 10 when their parents brought
them to Miami on a tourist visa sometime in the middle of June that
year. Angie and Meronie didn't think that they were going to stay in
Miami: their parents said that they would all go to the United States,
visit their "relatives,"[31] and then maybe see Disney World. The girls
were enjoying the visit in the U.S. and were not aware that their stay
would be more permanent until their parents enrolled them in the
local elementary school. They lived together in Miami until Christmas of that year. Their parents then sat them down, and had a conversation with them. As the girls tell me, their elderly, diabetic father
and poverty-worn mother told the girls that they loved them very
much, that they did the best that they ever could for them by bringing them to the United States, and that they would now return to
their home in Cap Haitian, Haiti. Meronie remembers giving Angie
a hug, telling her that she would take care of her, and that they would
be okay. They don't remember being angry at their parents, since they
agreed they had tried real hard.

One of the guidance counselors in Meronie's school, Ruth
McLean,[32] found out that the girls were living on their own and it
broke her heart. Ruth called her sister Mary in Hiawassee Springs –
who had been trying to conceive and had recently been dealt the news

---

31. These folks were nice enough, but turned out to be family friends without the time or means to raise their friends' kids.
32. Ruth was a delightful little spinster, about sixty years old. She never married, but she had the requisite four cats and a suspiciously good friend named
"Leslie" that she lived with. She also wore equally suspiciously comfortable shoes.

that she had two non-functioning ovaries and a lopsided uterus – and asked whether Mary would like to look after the girls, maybe even adopt them. Mary drove down to Miami to meet the girls, and she just fell in love. Meronie was too old to adopt for immigration purposes, having just passed the age of 16, but that Angie was still of age. The girls didn't feel right about having different last names, or one of them being adopted and not the other, so Mary became their "permanent guardian," but was "mom" in every other sense of the word.

The young sisters only came to my office because they heard that I could help. When I met them, Meronie was doing very well in school, all As and just a few Bs, despite working 10 hours a week at a fast food restaurant to send money home, speaking English as her second language, and helping to take care of her younger sister, who was not half the student that Meronie was. In addition to being their "mom," Mary McLean was also, like her sister, a guidance counselor at Hiawassee Springs High School. Mary, bless her sweet heart, just couldn't imagine loving Meronie more if she were her own child, and thought Meronie was the "county's prize pie." Her words, not mine. I kid you not. Anyway, sweet Mary had her heart and her head in the right place. After she realized that Meronie would qualify for financial assistance for college but could not apply because she lacked lawful immigration status, she got my number and called me at the IJC.

We talked for a while, and then she put Meronie on the phone. I was struck by how grown up she sounded, with only the slightest trace of an accent. We made an appointment for the following day after school. Meronie brought her sister, and they told me their story about how they had been brought from Haiti and abandoned. They didn't see it that way, but I knew that a judge might. Thankfully, our fine American Congress enacted the special immigrant juvenile (SIJ) provision of the Immigration and Nationality Act to assist undocumented immigrant children who have suffered parental abuse, abandonment or neglect. The enactment of that SIJ statute demonstrated the government's recognition that kids who have experienced various kinds of maltreatment in their families deserve special protection in the U.S. Given the unceremonious abandonment that Angie and Meronie suffered, and jumping through various legal and logistical hoops, we got the girls this special visa, and got them on their way to their chosen professions.[33]

When working with child clients, I constantly put on different hats, while navigating the bounds of legal ethics and professionalism. I probably hug my clients more than I should. In the interest of full disclosure: I hug the crap out of them. There, it's out there: may the authorities come and take me away. I use the fact that I don't look much older than them to my advantage, to try to forge a bond, and to have them trust me like their lawyer, and like their friend. I am their zealous advocate, and I hug them with zeal. That's just how it is.

Yesterday morning I got a call from a local private immigration lawyer. There are less than a handful of these characters in town, and each one of them barely ekes out a living. That said, these lawyers try to take on some pro bono cases while recognizing that they just can't afford to feed their families and make pro bono a large part of their already meager practices. Dan Thomas, one of the more colorful private immigration people in town, gave me a call yesterday morning. Dan likes to brag that he graduated very last in his class, but that he passed the bar, and so people still call him "lawyer." It wouldn't be my first go-to for a good joke, but he likes it.

So Dan calls, with a client in his office, and while she's in the room, he says, "Miss Lily," – which he really has no reason to call me, since Dan is a carpetbagger from less Southern places than North Florida – "I have a client here for you."

I sigh, inaudibly, since these "clients" that he has for me don't always have avenues for legitimate legal relief, and I usually spend more time giving bad news than good. I also hate to talk to potential clients about their potential immigration cases in front of Dan, or any other attorney for that matter. It reminds me of when my Dad used to ask me, "Doesn't your sister have beautiful hair?" I didn't think that Elena had beautiful hair – it was a pale blonde color, limp and straight – but I also didn't think the bounds of decency permitted me to tell the

---

33. Meronie wants to be a doctor, and to work with poor rural communities in Florida. After her experience in juvenile court and filing for her immigration status, Angie thinks she wants to be a public interest attorney. They say imitation is the most sincere kind of flattery.

truth. I knew that she envied my full-bodied auburn curls, even though I hated my hair, like almost every American teenage girl, growing up. When I was young, I didn't have the fortitude to confront my dad privately to ask him not to put me in that situation. I just knew that I shouldn't tell Elena that I thought her hair looked like dirty straw just stomped on by an angry albino horse. I mean, that's just not nice, right?

I have the same allergic reaction today to being asked, on the spot, whether I can assist a potential client on immigration matters. I also have more than a slight problem with conflict. This may be news to you, but I am not perfect. My flaws aside, or maybe because of them, I always tell Dan, "Just send them by my office."

Dan does, and within a matter of little more than an hour, potential clients show up at my friendly little office. Yesterday it was Osarobo, Osa for short. I always ask about an unusual name. I am sure you are curious as well. Amongst the Ebo people of Nigeria her name means "God is the magician or miracle worker." It was almost like she was making it up. I mean, I had never met someone more devout in the face of so little to believe in.

Ah, lovely Osa. Once she got over her disappointment that I was not an "older grown woman" and instead appeared to be "just a girl," she began to tell me her story. Her eyes brimmed with liquid, mascara smudging her cheeks, but she bit down on her lip, counted to five, and began her story again, this time without tears.

Osa had come to the United States from Nigeria ten years earlier. She came originally to New York to study at Columbia University, and had a legal student visa for her studies. She was studying religion, economics and studio art: Osa had many talents. Her four years in college breezed by. She studied, was very involved with her church, and worked several jobs as a waitress/dog walker/babysitter. She loved the freedom and excitement of New York City. Unfortunately, sometime during the frenetic busyness of college she stopped renewing her immigration status, so she had long been living in the U.S. without any real right to do so.

During those years, she had made many friends, but did not really go out on dates. She had only one secret crush, Robert, a fellow Nigerian who lived out of town, but who shared a commitment to her faith, and a strong friendship with her pastor. Their friendship grew over those nine years, and culminated in a surprising discussion for Osa.

One Autumn afternoon, seemingly out of the blue, Robert declared that she was the woman for him, that she had always been, but he had been too shy to admit it to her, afraid that she would reject him. He got down on one knee right there in Central Park, with the golden and red leaves descending upon them. He asked. She demurely, yet excitedly, agreed. They made plans: first a civil ceremony, and then a proper church wedding. By December they had done both, with traditional Ebo wedding garb and families from Nigeria in tow. Such bright colors, red and blue and gold and green. I got to see all the lovely pictures, big white smiles and vibrant fabric.

And then, the next month, they were off to start their married life together in Hiawassee Springs. Robert had a good job working as an architect with a local design firm. They arrived, and Robert drove Osa around town, showing her where all the important sites were. When they passed the mall, she asked to go in, and she saw a Banana Republic store, where she had worked in New York, and got an application for a job. She felt satisfied and excited that she was employable, and would not be a burden to her new husband. And so, Osa sold clothes for that first month at the Banana Republic, and she was the top seller that January. She was so successful that they asked her to apply for a managerial position. The only catch was that she didn't have her own car, and Robert grew tired of taking her to work. At first he continued to take her, albeit never on time and never when she asked. After a while, he just could not be bothered.

You see, Osa is a devout Christian, a true believer in marital harmony, and although she knew she would miss her job and financial independence, she conceded to Robert's wishes that she stop working and just stay home. Osa figured that instead of working outside the home, she would throw herself into all things domestic. She asked Robert if they could have some paint, so that she could clean up the mold-infested and decaying walls. He grew very angry at her suggestion, and refused to speak to her for a full week. Osa felt terrible for upsetting him. She tried again, about a week later, to ask him if she could do the grocery shopping, to make him nice meals every night when he came home from long days at the office. Again, he refused. He would do the shopping, and she would eat what he wanted her to eat.

She tried just one more time, a few months later, when she grew the courage to ask again for something that she needed. "Robert," she tried, with great trepidation, afraid of upsetting the already fraying blanket of marital harmony that she had tried to stitch each day, with loving words, and a devotion to their faith in God and each other. "Can I please borrow the car to go to church this evening? There is a bible study class, and it is too dark for me to be walking along the unpaved road in the evening. I am afraid that one of the cars won't see me. Please?" She knelt down before him, as he had asked her to do, and avoided his eyes, just using her voice to plead with him.

He flinched, as if punched in the chest by an invisible hand, but he didn't say a word. The following morning, Osa woke at around 6 a.m., and she noticed that Robert was not there. She thought, maybe, he had left early for work. She checked his closet, and thankfully, all of his clothes were there. She waited, patiently, in the house, all day for him, but even at 11 that night, he still hadn't appeared. She finally called the police, but they assured her that her husband would be home soon, and that they had to wait until he was missing for 48 hours before they would start searching for an adult. Osa was incredibly worried, and so she prayed with all her might that Robert would come home soon.

He never came home that night. Or the next. She tried calling him at the office, and his secretary told her that he could not be reached. She felt as if she would go mad. She consulted her pastor in New York, and the pastor she had met in Hiawassee Springs, and they told her to stay strong, and that they would send money if she needed it. She had $45 in her bank account, no way to get around, and th rent payment would soon be due. Where was Robert? Why would he do this to her? Had she not been a good wife? Maybe she had asked for too much, wanting to work, and to paint the apartment, and to use the car, and buy the food she wanted. She missed eating fish, and although she had asked Robert if he would buy some for her when he went shopping, he preferred turkey, so that's what they ate, and she tried to swallow it down, just like she did everything else, for the sake of the marriage.

Now Robert was gone. The weeks passed, each day almost equal to the next, with little distraction. She had a key to the apartment, but they lived in a gated apartment complex, and Robert refused to give her the plastic key pass to the gate. So, although he told her that she could leave the apartment whenever she wanted, he didn't encourage or facilitate it. After Robert had been gone three weeks and Osa had completely run out of food, she tried to leave the apartment complex. She soon discovered that she could not really come and go as she pleased but instead, she was dependent on a car entering the complex at the exact moment that she wanted to leave so that she could slip into and out of her cage, and flee to the local church for comfort and consolation. After almost a whole month had passed, the police and Robert appeared at her home one evening.

"Open up, ma'am, this is the police." Osa immediately feared the worst, thinking that they must have found Robert dead in a ditch somewhere. How else could she explain this odd behavior from her husband, a man she had known for almost a decade? She didn't want to open the door, she didn't want to know.

"Ma'am, please, open the door. This is the Hiawassee Springs Police Department. You must open the door." Again, Osa shrunk further into herself, slumped down by the couch near the front door.

"Ma'am, if you don't open up we are coming in. We can see you in there."

"Go away," Osa said, inaudibly, to herself, inside her screaming head. "I want you to go away."

The police bolted through the door, one large mustached man, the other, thin, pale and young, looked scared himself. "Robert Ndole has sent us here to collect his belongings" reported the large one.

"Does that mean he isn't dead?" Osa cried true tears of happiness. "My husband is still alive! Thank you, Jesus!" She exclaimed, full of hope and promise, her Christian forgiveness in full force, her overstimulated mind already spinning for the glorious life they would rebuild and share together.

"Um, ma'am, Mr. Ndole is outside with a moving truck. He wanted us here in case you tried to stop him. He would like to enter and gather his things without any kind of disturbance."

Osa could barely comprehend this man. She spoke perfect English, so it wasn't a language barrier. This man was saying incomprehensible things. Disturbance? "Robert was my husband," she said to herself inside her head. "He is my husband."

"Robert is my husband, officer, what kind of disturbance do you mean? I'm so happy that he is alive and back home with me, where he belongs."

At that point, Robert stepped over the threshold of the apartment, into their home, and standing in front of a large wedding picture of the two of them, said with a completely straight face, "This woman is not my wife. Officer, I need to get my things and go."

"Robert, what do you mean? Please don't do this. I've missed you. I am your wife. I need you, I love you. I am your wife. Please don't go."

Robert stepped around Osa's open arms as if she were a piece of discarded old furniture and the officers ignored her pleadings. Robert did his best to convince the policemen that Osa was not the glorious woman in the wedding picture, with a gold headdress and brightly colored clothes. Given Osa's current state of disrepair, and perhaps their desire to believe Robert (finding the situation too implausible otherwise), they helped him pack his things, and left Osa the number of a local homeless shelter, in case she needed a place to go.

Hearing her accent, and coming to the realization that she was not originally from Hiawassee Springs, Florida, the smaller and younger of the two gentlemen walked over to her.

"Ma'am, I can see that you are not from around these parts. I can also see that maybe this man is your husband, maybe he ain't. Either way, you might need some help. Try calling this number. There is a woman there named Miss Lily who might be able to help." This slight uniformed man pressed my card into her palm.[34]

Within a few days' time, her pastors had wired her enough money to make rent for the month, and enough extra cash to rent a car just a few days a week. Osa came to my office, looking like a fine profes-

---

34. Thankfully, I had met with all of the law enforcement officers in the area to talk about the kind of immigration law that I practice during my first month at the IJC. They were happy to make inroads with the otherwise closed off immigrant community and I was happy to have the backup, especially for my clients in situations of domestic violence.

sional lady ready to shop – not simply to work – at a place like Banana Republic. Funny, that, the need to look the part of wherever you work. My dad used to be amused at the "highfalutin"[35] attitude that folks who worked at fancy stores would take, like Tiffany's and Coach and the like. They acted as if it wouldn't take a month of their salary to afford little items in that store and treated the customers with privileged disdain. My dad really hated those salespeople.

But Osa was different. She carried herself with a flowing dignified grace. We explored her options for immigration relief. I told her about something called VAWA, which stands for the Violence Against Women Act. Sometime within the last decade Congress had the good sense to protect women in Osa's situation. They gave Osa the ability to petition for her own immigration status, so that she doesn't have to depend on a physically or emotionally abusive spouse to get around to doing it. Despite all his faults, Robert at least didn't hold the carrot of immigration status above Osa's head. He simply left her alone, with no means of income or transportation, isolated from friends and family, with no key with which to leave the prison he created for her.

We got Osa a key. She is going to be fine. Her name, Osa, is also the name of a Peninsula off the coast of Costa Rica where I once took a trip with my friend Elise. We boarded a tiny craft to embark on our adventure to that remote island with the diverse and mysterious ecosystem. We got cheap tickets to Costa Rica, which we discovered later were such a good bargain because it was the rainy season. The seas were rough and it took four times the usual measure to land our craft. We had two local Ticos navigating for us, and they seemed to manage the boat better when they had acquired more of our money. I would have given them everything I owned and hoped to ever get in the future if they would just get us to dry land. Elise and I spent the night in what would have been a very romantic locale for two, had

___

35. Yes, ladies and gents, my dad was originally from the South. He was born in Memphis, and lived there till he was about 10 years old and his family decided they had enough of all things Southern. I've always liked the few, leftover expressions my dad held onto from his childhood, which is probably why I cottoned to the people and their expressions in Hiawassee Springs. It does feel a bit like coming home.

we been romantically involved, and not two old friends alone in a bungalow built for honeymooners. I digress, only to say that Osa is a name that to me, means daring and adventuresome, but possibly a bit misguided. As Osa and I discussed her various options, she adamantly told me that there would be no divorce. That she and Robert and their families did not in any way believe in divorce. Osa was waiting for Robert to come home, and she held fast to this belief, despite all evidence to the contrary.

I deeply respected Osa's adherence to her faith, which gave her strength to move forward, to find solutions. I held Osa's hands and hugged her as we parted, trying to imbibe some of that strength through osmosis. Osa needed my help, and I would give it to her. I would not be shutting down the IJC. I knew then that I would operate without money if I needed to, and that I would trust, just like Osa did, against all odds, that something would work out for us.

Chapter 16

Rosa

Querida Diary,

I am sorry that I haven't written in so long. I know that I must write, both to practice my English and to recount my experiences, so that one day when I leave I can go back to school and not be so far behind. Sometimes, though, it is just too much to write all of this down. I am ashamed to admit, but I have thought, more than once, about taking my own life. I could only tell you this, no one else. Each time, I thought only of three people: Mami, Ana and Maria. I know that Mami would be devastated if we never saw each other again, especially after losing Papi. I know that she misses running her hands down my long, smooth hair as much as I miss feeling her warm hands on my head at night. I know it would be too much for Maria to lose both Papi and me, and to have to care for Mami alone. Whenever it feels like too much and I start feeling dead inside, I think of Ana's smile and her laugh. I try to imagine something that she would do to make me laugh. I try to remember her frog puppet. It helps to lift my spirits, which are down and dark most of the time.

I felt like writing because something out of the ordinary happened, and I wanted to make sure that I remembered, so that I could remind myself that possibilities might exist – even if one day far far into the future when I have paid off my debts – that are outside this current life I find myself in.

Things with the Cuencas have definitely gotten worse since I last wrote. *My biggest worry had been that Martin would try to do to me what he did to Ana, but gracias a dios, he hasn't much bothered with me at all. Instead, the problem is with his parents in the house, Señor y Señora Cuenca. I hate them both very much.*

The Cuencas barely speak to me now, and they don't have me working in their restaurant at all. Instead, I take care of the home. I still wake very early in the morning, but now I never leave the house. I cook breakfast for everyone, clean up, and then am allowed to eat only the scraps of whatever is left over, and I have to do it in my room, instead of in the kitchen like the rest of the family. After the family heads to work, sometimes Martin lags behind to make sure that I am dusting and vacuuming the way he thinks is right. I spend all day cleaning the house and preparing the meals for them. In the afternoon, Señor y Señora Cuenca return for something to eat. Whether it is salad and lentejas or salchicon or arroz con pollo, it is always too something. Señora Cuenca finds my food too bland, la Señora says it's too salty, and Martin always thinks there isn't enough, which means that often, there aren't any leftovers at all for me to eat. It's okay, though, because I don't feel like eating after making the meal, watching them eat and hearing them complain and cleaning up, se quita las ganas, sabes? I just don't have the appetite.

I then continue to clean the house, do laundry, mop the floors. They are such pigs. Señora Cuenca's black hairs cling to the walls of the shower and the tub, like trails of her evilness, everywhere I look. They come home at the end of the day, and it is the same routine with the food again. I serve them, and the croquetas are too fried or too breaded, or the empanadas too hot or the churrasco undercooked. Again, often once Martin is done feeding his big belly there is nothing left for me. They lock the pantry when I am home alone so I cannot steal their food. Sometimes I sneak pieces of their discarded food before it goes in the garbage just to calm the loud hunger in my stomach.

I can hear the television from the other room loud in my bedroom, but I am not permitted to watch it. Instead, I just overhear. It helps my imagination to wonder what the characters look like and how they carry themselves. I put on plays in my head with the voices I hear from the television movies and shows.

The days and weeks pass, almost always the same, which is why, *me quita las ganas* to write—what is there to say? It is all the same.

One thing happened worthy of sharing, though, a very different thing. You remember I told you about the showers? How the Cuencas stopped letting me take hot showers? I hated taking those cold showers. Well, the shower situation got worse and the Cuencas got even more mean about it. They would tease me, and call me bad names for being "india," and would say that my people were dirty and didn't need to shower. They told me that my showers were costing them too much money. One day, I went in to take a quick cold shower. I had finished undressing and turned on the water when Señor Cuenca quietly opened the door, took his clothes off and followed me in. I was terribly scared. I asked him, politely, to leave and to please give me my privacy. He said, "This is my house and you will follow my rules and you are not paying your fair share to live here. You will do as I say."

I panicked, not having any idea what to do. I knew that Señora Cuenca had left the house just minutes before to go grocery shopping, which is why I went to quickly shower, before she returned with the items I would need to arrange in the cabinets.

"Please, Señor Cuenca," I said, "I am a good girl. I will do more chores, I can work more at the restaurant, but please, please. . . ."

He grabbed at my right breast and pinched my nipple roughly.

"Tonight, india, I will just watch you take a shower, and see how the india wastes all of our money, flushing it down the drain. Go ahead. Let's see."

You can imagine that I didn't want him to see me naked, but I felt like I had no choice. I must have stayed in that freezing water with that horrible man for only two minutes, but it felt like forever. As I went to grab my towel and cover up to exit the shower, I heard Señora Cuenca's car pulling up, and Señor Cuenca ran out of the shower as fast as his fat devil legs could carry him. Phew, I was relieved.

I have a bad feeling about the shower now, since Señor Cuenca watched me in there. I try to use the shower only when he is not home, but even still: I feel like I am dirty and I cannot get clean. It has been unbearably hot and humid, and because the Cuencas are too cheap to pay for air conditioning, I walk around the house all day in a thin sticky sweat that stays until I am permitted to shower. A few weeks ago, while the Cuencas were all at the restaurant, I decided to head into the small backyard where I manage the plants and do the gardening, and shower there, instead, in the outdoors, where I feel free, and where the heat of the day was likely to make the water a bit warmer than the freezing cold shower inside. That first time that I wandered outside for a hose-shower, I did so with great trepidation, only keeping the water on for a few seconds before I shut it off and ran into the house, shaking like a wet dog. Now, I venture out to the backyard a few times a week, strip down to my underwear and soap up, breathe in the fresh air, see the sun, smell the neighbor's fresh cut grass and feel a little of the joys of life I used to know.

Yesterday, I was taking a hose-shower in the backyard when I caught someone spying on me. I saw a flash of orange, and some blue jeans, and I heard a rustle in the bushes, the kind that didn't seem to come from a squirrel or a bird, but from a sneaky human. I thought it must be Señor Cuenca, and that something terrible was going to happen. I ran inside, soaking the carpet with my soapy feet, too numb to move, in a state of panic.

I waited. I waited a few more minutes. Nothing happened. Nothing happened until around 2 p.m. that day, when I was serving the Cuencas their almuerzo or afternoon lunch meal when there was a knock at the door.

"Police, open up please."

In a flash I saw a side of Señora Cuenca that I hadn't since her appearance in Jujuy. She gathered up her hair into a tidy updo, plastered on a smile, and graciously opened the door. Almost instinctively, I went to hide in the bathroom. I couldn't hear or understand much of the conversation that followed between Señora Cuenca and the police officer, but I imagine it went something like this.

"Well hello, officer, how do you do?" Her tone sounded very proper, as if he had come over on official business to have an important meal. I hated her very much at that moment.

"I'm fine, thanks. I need to talk to you about something. Your neighbor reported seeing a young girl showering with a hose in your backyard. Do you have a daughter?"

Without skipping a beat, as if she actually expected the question, she replied, "A daughter? Oh, you must mean Rosa. Yes, of course I have a daughter. She is not completely right in the head, so she never learned to speak proper English, but she is mine."

"Señora, why wasn't Rosa at school on a Thursday morning?"

"Officer, the class had a special trip that day to an art museum, and Rosa couldn't go because she wouldn't have understood any of the instruction about the paintings."

I peeked out from my door to see what was going on. I didn't understand much of what was going on, but I could tell that the officer was suspicious. He raised an eyebrow at Señora Cuenca.

"Can I see her birth certificate, Señora Cuenca?"

At that point, I wandered out of the bathroom and over to the rest of the Cuencas, sitting and standing awkwardly around the officer.

"Are you Rosa?" he asked me, kindness and concern all over his face. I thought about what to do for a second. The Cuencas had told me, over and over again, that I was only allowed to stay in the United States because they had told people that I was their daughter. They told me that the police are corrupt, and that they hate immigrants, and that if I told them that I had lied, and that I wasn't actually their daughter, they would throw me in jail, and I would never see Mami again. I thought for a second, but I knew what I had to do.

"Jes, I yam Rosa." I said, in the best English I could manage.

The officer tried speaking to me in Spanish, which did not sound like his first language, and I didn't trust him, despite his kind face.

"Por que estabas duchando en la yarda?" the officer tried. He asked me why I was showering in the backyard. I told him it was because I liked being in the water outside, which I hoped sounded believable, like something a fourteen year old girl living in America would do. I did not want to go to jail, and I needed to see Mami again, even if wouldn't be until far into the future.

At that moment, Señora Cuenca returned with my passport. I didn't bring my birth certificate with me from Jujuy, so I knew she didn't have it.

"Officer, here is the passport for my daughter, Rosa Cuenca. We all have both American and Argentinean passports, it makes travel much easier. As you can see, she just recently turned fourteen, and we had a lovely birthday party for our sweet, little Rosa."

The truth was that my birthday had recently passed, but there certainly wasn't a party. I don't remember doing anything special at all, or anyone taking notice.

The officer spent time looking through the passport, flipping through the empty pages. He looked very young and I wondered how long he had been an officer and what kind of training he had.

"Es la verdad, Rosa? Las Cuencas son tus padres? Y normalmente vas a la escuela?" He asked whether all that Señora Cuenca said was true, that the Cuencas were my parents, and that I usually go to school. I wanted to scream, "No!" from the top of my lungs, but I knew better. I knew that if I said anything different, that I could go to jail or worse, and then I would never pay off my debt, and the Cuencas might go after Maria to work in my place. They had told me as much. They told me that if I ever tried to run away, that they would get Maria to live with them, and that she would share a room with Martin. Just like Ana. I couldn't do that to little Maria, not after what had happened to Ana, not after the life I was leading.

"Sí, Señor, es la verdad." Yes, I told the young officer, it is true. All of it is true. I hated to lie, but I knew it was best for everyone I loved if I did.

The officer looked at each one of us, searching for an answer as to what he should do. His shrug of the shoulders seemed to suggest to the Cuencas that he was sorry to bother them about nothing, they smiled in response, and then he said goodbye to us and closed the door.

I felt alive during those moments that the officer was in the house. I had no idea what might happen, but I knew, during those minutes, that the possibility existed that I could leave the Cuencas. At that moment in time, jail seemed a better option that staying with them. I think that what kept me from turning myself over completely was the possibility that I would be replaced with Maria. I couldn't do that to my little sister. Mami could not lose first Papi, and then both of us. I knew that, for Mami's sake, I needed to lie, and I needed to stay, to pay off the debt that I owed, and I hoped that in time I would be forgiven for all that I had done wrong.

As soon as the door closed and the officer was far enough away, the Cuencas began to beat me. Señora Cuenca looked me straight in the eye, and told me how stupid I was to shower in the backyard where people would see me, and know that I must be an animal, because only animals showered outside. Then, she spat into my face.

Señora Cuenca was the most cruel of the Cuencas, and that was saying a lot, because her husband and son were bad people. La Señora punched me over and over again in the stomach, so that, she said, "No one will see your bruises." Señora Cuenca pulled at my hair until my scalp bled and Martin even got in on the beating and slapped my face while calling me "stupid" and "ugly" and terrible, terrible names. At some point during the beating, I lost consciousness.

But I am here, Diary, I keep on going.

Till next time,

Rosa

Chapter 17

Mila

I didn't want to bother Chico about my visa again, but I was starting to worry. A few months had passed since that awful day when Jose tried to make me have sex with him and Chico reassured me that he would take care of my visa. It was possible that he had already taken care of it, and that with everything else he has to do, he just hadn't mentioned it to me yet. I didn't want to bother him by asking him again, but all day long I thought about the visa, and I made up my mind that I would ask him about it that night after work.

It was our usual nightly routine. Jose drove us all home, texting as he drove, his eyes barely on the road, and once back at the apartment, Chico and I went to his room and made love. I decided to ask him then, when I was sure that he was relaxed and in a good mood, about my visa.

"Chico, my love, I am sorry to bother you with such boring things after such an exciting time with my man, but I want to stay here in America with you as long as possible. How are things going with my visa?"

"Oh Mila, I have also been wanting to talk to you about the visa for a long time. I know that your dream is to become a famous actress, and with that face and that body," he ran his rough hands over my smooth white skin and sighed, "I know you will go far. I think it is time for you get more experience in the industry, you know, performing."

"Oh Chico, I would love that. I can do so many different roles, accents, and I can change my look to fit many different types. Are you thinking we should move to New York? I hope so, I really think New York is the place to …" He put one gentle finger over my mouth and laughed.

"Oh Mila, let's not get ahead of ourselves. Sure, we will go to New York, together, one day. For now, let's just focus on getting you some experience. This is about your visa, too. Hunan is doing well, but still

Jose and I barely make a living. I have been supporting you, housing you, keeping you fed and happy," he touched my breasts one at a time and we laughed together, "but I can only keep doing this for so long at this rate. I need you to be making more of a contribution to our finances."

"But Chico," I tried giving him my most winsome face, "I am already working seven days a week, and so many hours each day, I don't know if I can do much more."

"Mila, I was thinking maybe you could take on a different kind of work, to help pay your debt off faster, and to help you prepare for your acting career." I had to admit, it sounded great. I wanted to get to New York, preferably with Chico, as fast as I could, and it seemed like only this debt was really standing in my way.

"Ooo, that sounds great, Chico, tell me more." I playfully slid a hand across his broad, hairy chest.

"Good girl, Mila. During the day tomorrow, I will get you some things for your new job, and then tomorrow night, we'll leave work a little early, check out the place, and you'll meet the owner and decide if it's the right work for you."

I was pleased and tired, and we fell asleep in each other's arms. We woke early the following morning, and headed to work. Jose and Chico entered through one door, and me through the back entrance with the other employees. The day could not have gone by fast enough for me. I even tried to imagine the theatre group that I would work with during the evenings, but I couldn't. I wondered if we would do Shakespeare! I had never really thought about doing stage acting, I mean, I have a face that is really meant more for close-ups on the big screen, but I guess any acting experience was good while I was still trying to pay my way to New York City.

I saw Chico out of the corner of my eye and he made an upward motion with his head. That motion usually meant that I should meet him for some "quality time" in the closet, but today I knew that it meant something different. I was so excited!

Jose stayed at Hunan to watch over things and Chico and I left at about 8 p.m. to head to my first real acting job. I was bubbling over with excitement. Sitting in the passenger seat, I just kept looking at Chico, smiling goofily, touched that he made the special effort to help me find an extra job doing acting work. I knew then for sure that he wanted for me to be free of debt so that I could follow my own dreams and we could move on with our lives together.

"I love you," I told him, then and there, for the first time.

"Okay Mila, let's not get carried away." He smiled, though, and I think he meant that he loved me, too. It's just that he's a big macho guy, and his culture doesn't permit him to be as open with his affections. I know how he feels by the way he holds me at night, and because he chooses me to be with him, when there are many other nice girls at work, and other girls that he probably meets. He chooses me.

"Let's go inside, Mila." And we did. We went into the VIP Club of Atlanta. It was dark, and there were a few beautiful women walking around in sexy outfits carrying drinks and talking to men.

Chico asked to speak to a man named Sebastian. Sebastian arrived a few minutes later and he and Chico spoke in Spanish, while smiling at me. Chico translated for me and told me that Sebastian was pleased with how beautiful I am. I smiled. Sebastian would choose me for this role, I knew it.

Chico gave me the bag that he had been carrying and we went into the back to change. I looked in the bag and smiled at Chico.

"Chico, are we doing a production of Chicago? I saw that one. Am I going to be the older woman who kills her husband or the new one? Oh, I bet I'm the new one, because she's blonde. It's a great role!" I was really excited, and put on the stiletto heels, black thigh high stockings with a matching garter belt and g-strings. The top was also a lacy black push up bra with some red tassels attached. I have to say, I looked great.

"Wow, Mila, you look fantastic," Chico said with admiration. "My girl is a sexy lady," he said as he patted me on my bottom. "I can't wait to take you home tonight."

"Are you going to stay and watch me rehearse?" I asked, already not caring much whether he stayed or not. I was going to be an actress and this was my first role!

"No, Mila, I'll go, but I'm sure Sebastian and the other girls will show you the ropes."

Chico left and within minutes two other girls entered the room. One girl, Britney, was from Kentucky and the other girl, Katie, was originally from Russia. They told me that I would be serving drinks to customers and that I could keep any tips that I made. They told me how much to charge for each drink, how to stand and sit, and that if the customers wanted "more" that they would need to pay for it.

"You mean more drinks?" I asked, naively, wondering whether we just served drinks until the actual show rehearsal started.

They laughed, I think assuming that I was kidding. Britney told me how things worked around the VIP "Mila, you seem like a nice girl, so I am going to give it to you straight. We work in shifts. After we finish serving drinks for a while, it becomes our turn to dance on the stage. You don't have to take off any of your clothes, but you are not likely to make very much money if you don't. Make them pay for each thing you remove, don't you go givin' nothin' away for free here."

"I don't understand, Britney. Aren't we doing a production of Chicago tonight?"

Again, Britney and Katie laughed, thinking that I was pulling on their legs.

"Sure, Mila, it's Chicago, 'cept here in Atlanta the performance is a little different," Britney slapped her thigh, thinking she had just made a very funny joke.

Katie must have noticed then, that I actually wasn't joking. She sat next to me, and put her hand gently on my leg, "Mila, I promise you it is a nice way to make money. You can make so much money in one night you wouldn't believe. Last weekend I made over $1000 just in tips, and your body is even nicer than mine. You are a very pretty girl, and you will do well."

It was not what I expected, but don't all actresses suffer for their craft? I knew that I could use this experience sometime in the future, if I ever had to play that actress in *Striptease* I could do it with real grit. Besides, where was I going to go? Chico was my ride and he had left. I might as well go through with it for one night and see what happens.

I served drinks, having to endure one or two more slaps and pats to my backside than I felt comfortable with. Britney, Katie and I were part of a shift. When we were done serving drinks, the three of us got up on stage, and I did my best to seem like a real stripper. The men, drunk and sloppy though they were, went wild for me. It was actually kind of fun. After receiving some money from one man, I decided to really get into the part and to take off my top. I leaned over to one of the men and put my breasts in his face. He put a $100 bill in his teeth and I took it from him with mine. More bills came, more clothing went, and within thirty minutes I was wearing nothing but heels and my killer smile, with $900 more to my name. I tried to – not obviously – search the audience for Chico, but it was dark, and there were bright lights on me. Still, I didn't see him anywhere. When we were done it was about two in the morning, and I waited outside with the other girls for their rides. Chico showed up, just like I knew he would, and he got outside of the car to open my door. The other girls were definitely jealous of what a nice man I had found for myself.

I said goodnight to Britney and Katie and got into the car.

"So, Mila, how much did you make?" Chico asked with a smile and a raised eyebrow.

"Chico, it was incredible. I made over $100 in tips for serving drinks and another $900 for my dancing. I made more than $1000 tonight." I fanned out all the money in front of him, and smiled coyly over the money-fan.

I could tell that Chico was happy with me. He smiled broadly.

"That's my girl," he said. "You know, some of that money has to go back to Sebastian for giving you a chance at this job. We will bring him back 25 percent, so tonight let's set aside $250 for him."

I pouted and frowned, "But I did all the work, Chico."

"Yes, love, but he gave you, a girl from some nowhere place in Europe, a chance even though you have never performed before. We owe him at least that much."

"Okay," I said, taking Chico's free hand in mine as we drove the rest of the way home. Chico was in a kinky mood and wanted me to put on the Chicago outfit again for him, and to dance for him the way I danced for the other men. I complied, putting on a show for the second time that night.

"I'm so glad you were able to make so much money, Mila. I haven't wanted to bother you about it, but your debt is really racking up, and I need you to pitch in some more. Are you okay with going back to the VIP and making more money for us, Mila?"

"Of course, love, I will do that for us." I wanted so badly to please

Chico and to get to New York as soon as possible. It felt nearer now than ever before.

I didn't know that Chico meant that I should work at the club every night and the Hunan every day. I did it, for him, to pay off my debts, but it was extremely exhausting. I barely slept, and the alcohol I consumed when customers insisted that I share drinks with them started to weigh on me. I had trouble falling asleep, and when I did, my dreams were fitful, always something of Mother, and occasionally I could see my father's face float in and out. My dreams imitated my life. My former one, not this new life in Atlanta.

Chapter 18

Lily

I still haven't talked to Josh about the Cornell letter. I have, however, exploded at him for a million other reasons that have nothing to do with his impending dash for the North. He has been yelled at for leaving his socks by the bed, forgetting to close the bathroom door so that I felt cold while taking a shower, and accidentally setting the alarm clock twenty minutes ahead so that I got less sleep than I wanted. I have yelled at him for everything but what is really going on. I am scared that Josh, my thoughtful, quiet, and measured Josh, might be looking at exit options.

I feel like there is a distance growing between us, one that I might be causing with all of my arguments over nothing, and I don't like it. I tend to argue over stupid minutiae but avoid real conversations about what is actually bothering me like it's the bubonic plague.[36] Josh is also not an extremely confrontational person, which means when things go wrong (which they haven't ever before, but we didn't know each other that well before we got married), I don't really know how we'll go about solving them. What is still getting at me, though, is that I am not ready to have children yet, and I just can't explain away that feeling. Could it be about Josh? What is it that keeps me from wanting to move forward with our life as a family?

---

36. See what I mean about my flair for drama. Why can't I just say, "I tend to avoid conflict with others" or "I try to avoid conflict at all costs?" Years of therapy have taught me that in situations like this it is best to blame my mother, so I will. Here goes. I must have inherited this propensity toward the dramatic from my mother, Diana Walker. She was often afraid that we would fall on a toy left in the middle of the room because it would cause us to "break our necks," the most likely and incurable of injuries. Or, there was the Walker family favorite of "put on socks or you'll catch your death." The conclusion there is an obvious one: not wearing socks while walking on a hard floor will automatically lead to the death of young children. Is it any wonder?

The complicated truth is that I feel guilty complaining about anything when my clients' lives are so hard. Instead of appreciating Josh for all he is, I feel guilty for having a loving husband that doesn't abuse me.[37] I feel guilty for complaining about having to live in a town I didn't choose when my clients choose love and it bites them in the face. I feel guilty for my easy ride when my clients have to make Sisyphean efforts just to keep safe and alive. At times, I feel like I could drown, face first, in puddles of my own guilt.

Guilt aside, the simple answer for why I am not ready for children is my clients. I keep whatever professional distance is required by the Florida Rules on Ethics and Professional Responsibility, but hey, it is hard not to hug them to pieces sometimes. Sure, we provide legal services for free, and sure, they couldn't pay us even if they wanted to, but they find other ways to compensate me for my time. One of my clients made homemade enchiladas for me after I had missed a day of work due to a nasty little stomach virus. Another gave me a birthday present of chocolates and a clear plastic bear with angel wings that she painted green eyes on to look like me, and she called it her *"Abogada* Lily-Bear." Once I had a good Samaritan neighbor bring in a battered woman in need, and to thank me for providing legal services for his friend, he sent me a CD of Christian music that he had recorded, as well as a paperback copy of his self-published work on the mysteries of the great beyond.[38] The enchiladas were definitely the tastier option, but I hadn't laughed so hard as I did when I saw Craig's self titled book, "Craig Wayne Johnston Unlocks the Secrets to the Universe."

My sweet clients. I know that if I do not provide them with legal representation, they may have no other options. That reality weighs

---

37. And I do appreciate that Josh doesn't actively abuse me. But I do wonder sometimes if he understands me at all. He talks about how much he loves me, and he certainly is affectionate, but I constantly wonder whether he just needed someone to come with him to Hiawassee Springs and whether I just seemed like the most willing idiot. He is withdrawn, he never wants to talk about our relationship, and sometimes I feel like I don't know him any better now than on the day we met.

38. I tried to get Josh to assign it to his freshman English class, but he wasn't feeling it.

heavily on me. That notion of being needed at work is new and different for me. I used to spend even more hours working than I do now,
but I wasn't personally invested. I would leave work and trot around
Dupont Circle, lingering for hours with friends over mango mojitos,
digesting every last bit of the conversations we shared regarding our
potential future boyfriends. I spent countless hours over the last five
years going on dates, preparing for dates, and debriefing about the
dates with each of my many friends in D.C. I don't do that anymore,
and undoubtedly my life is richer as a consequence. I have Josh now,
and I care so much more about my job that there isn't much left over
to gab about – with him or anyone else – when the day is through.

I was nonchalantly looking through the thin "Things to Do" in the
"About Town" section of the Hiawassee Springs Gazette last week
when I found the key to how Josh and I would climb out of our first
slump. There it was, in all its splendor, the perfect text alongside a
picture of a really happy pig, wearing a cowboy hat and a big grin.
That's right, ladies and gents, the Eighty-Second Annual Northwest
Florida County Fair. Sweet![39]

"Josh, Josh, Josh, look!" I grabbed the paper, happy pig picture
emblazoned front and center, and ran over to Joshua, thrusting the
paper on top of the stack of student papers he was grading. He did-
n't really have much choice but to read the selection.

"Can we go? Can we go? Can we go?" I playfully tugged on the
right sleeve of his worn thin grey T-shirt that I had inherited eons ago
from an ex-boyfriend and passed on to Josh because it looked better
on him.[40]

"Sure, Lily," he replied, without even one one hundred thousandth
of the same level of enthusiasm that I showed. "The fair goes on for
ten days, I'm sure we can find a day when we can go together." He
sounded like he was trying to make me happy, but not like he really
cared to go on his own. I felt instantly crushed, like a little girl on a

---

39. I am doing a double fist pump gesture, which you, unfortunately, can't
see right now, but if you could, you would better understand my feeling of cel-
ebration. The power of words can only take us just so far.

40. Um, I kind of never told Josh the true origins of that shirt. Why ruin his
enjoyment of a perfectly nice T-shirt?

family road trip who tries and tries to get the large truck driver racing alongside their station wagon to honk his big, loud horn and the driver sees the little girl, and knows what she wants, but he refuses. I felt crushed like that little girl[41] felt crushed.

Still, a few days later, after a long hard week, we went to the fair on a Friday night. I loved the excess of the fair, and the sheer insanity. The sun was setting as we arrived and I made it my goal to eat just enough so that I would be sickeningly full, but not too sick to actually prevent me from going on the Turbonator, and not so sick as to actually vomit. It was a precarious balance, especially as I danced my way from the fried Oreos[42] to the stir-fried okra to the other fried delicacies of the evening: candy bars, brownies, and peanut butter cups. Josh had a lemonade. One lemonade. He was not embracing the caloric extravagance with the same tenacity I dedicated to trying to acquire Type II Diabetes. That very evening.

The fair was, in a word, awesome. They had five different species of roosters. The animal room had local sheep, chickens and pigs, and then some imported varieties of animalia which were very pleasing to me. The following were present: the alpaca, the llama, and the Highland Cow.[43] After we (well, more like I) played with the animals for a while, we watched some barely-semi-professional glee club singers do a mix of singing and clogging for as long as we could possibly stand.[44]

---

41. Yeah, okay fine, I was that little girl. What kind of sick person would refuse a cute little girl's wishes to hear a loudly honked horn? That day, the one without a loud honk, was the day I learned that the world would not always be a friendly place.

42. Don't you dare judge me.

43. This animal hails from Scotland and has a most pleasing hairdo involving a gentle forward comb of the mane, between the ears and over the snout. Occasionally I like to comb Josh's hair this way, and when he is feeling charitable, he will allow this coiffure and say it in the Scottish accent which sounds like, "Moo, I'm uh Highland Coo!" It is adorable.

44. For the record, I lasted 6.5 minutes, Josh skipped out at 3 minutes flat to "um, use the bathroom." I found his excuse specious at best. The Hiawassee Springs Town singers were awesome. Kind of. For their genre. Whatever genre that was, which was unclear.

At approximately 8:30 for the 9 p.m. showing of the eighty-second annual pig races, the crowd gathers. Words cannot describe the joy on a young Hiawassee Springsian child's face upon seeing his first pig race. It is magical. This year, Tammy Faye Bacon beat out David Letterham, which is only fair, given the real Tammy Faye's struggles with cancer. She deserved to win at something. The first few rounds were just your average pig racing: pretty standard really. Four pigs would race around their straw-laden rings while the people would bet on who would finish first. The last round brought the throng of tired fair-goers to their feet. Suspense built. And there they were: potbellied pigs! Joshua even smiled at this one, quiet as he was all evening. He even laughed out loud when one of the four pigs just stopped in its tracks and sat on his chubby pig hindquarters while the others waddled aimlessly around the ring.

"Josh, lately I feel as lost as that pig."

"Which pig, Lilybillygoat?" Josh asked mockingly, he knew exactly which pig. I smiled anyway, though. He hadn't called me that in too long. I felt a break in the tension that had been hanging between us for months, ever since Josh first mentioned us having kids.

Josh smiled deeper then, kind of a nervous smile, the corner twitching up at the left side of his mouth, but the right just couldn't get on board. He took a deep, long sigh.

"Lily. It's just that when we agreed to get married you said you were turning a new leaf and going to put us before work." Josh exhaled slowly. "And now, I don't know, things are different. I mean, I want you to love your work. I just want you to love me more."

Where was this coming from? It wasn't a conversation to have with all those screaming pig fans around us. Or maybe it was. Either way, I loved that man, I saw that he was in pain, and I wanted to be in our home together. I didn't care that our home was still filled with cockroach dung or that we had weird landlords. I just wanted to go home.

I grabbed into his pocket for the keys, gestured towards the exit, and he gratefully followed, our fingers linked. He had endured as much of the fair as he could possibly take, and he had done it for me.

We drove without talking for the whole ride home. It was twenty minutes, filled with country music, which was all that played from the local radio stations at that hour. They were playing that week's top song entitled something like, "Honkey Tonk Bdonk adonk."[45] We pulled onto the dimly lit dirt path that doubled for our driveway, and walked hand in hand into our house. We made love that night, with a familiar tenderness, and a new sense of purpose and excitement. We didn't use any kind of birth control or protection, my way of saying that I agreed. It was time. I wasn't scared then. I wanted him to know that I did value our family, more than anything, that his happiness was mine. We fell asleep in each other's arms, both comforted in a way we hadn't been in way too long.

In the light of the morning, things felt very different than they did even the night before. I got up, threw on some clothes, made some coffee, and began pacing the house like an expectant father. What the f**k was I thinking? I took two sips of the coffee, and then spat it into the sink.

"I might be pregnant, so no more coffee for me," I said to myself, already irritated that Josh gets to keep drinking coffee and I don't. Not even 24 hours possibly pregnant and I was already getting a little nutty. I poured the rest of the coffee from my "Famous Women And Their Important Sayings About Life" mug (that my mom had given me during a rough, lonely time in my life) into the stained sink and took a deep, long breath in and out. I decided to try talking to Josh about my thoughts and fears, since we had joined up to face life together.

I padded into our bedroom, "Good morning, Joshycito," I said, mussing his sandy brown hair, kissing him on the forehead, grudgingly nudging some black liquid caffeine in his direction. No milk, two sugars.

He woke with half-closed eyes, wrinkling up his face as if disturbed that a new day had to go on and start without him. Once even just a little bit conscious, he smiled at me, eyes still closed, made some sort of happy grunting sound and motioned for me to come back to bed with him. I sat down next to him on the bed.

"Why dressed?" was all he could manage to get out. Josh was not a morning person. "Come back to bed" He was trying to be as cute

---

45. Clearly a classic in the making.

as he could be, but that morning, it was definitely not working. I put
his mug of coffee on the stained old oak end table next to our bed
and crawled back into bed with him. He quickly fell back asleep and
I tried to do the same. I wasn't sure if it was the two sips of caffeine
that made my heart race, or the idea that I might have gotten pregnant the night before. I suddenly felt like I was going to vomit, and I
ran to the bathroom to pay homage to the porcelain bowl. As I stood
there for a few moments, I didn't feel nauseated in the slightest. I realized that I was just being silly. I scooted back to bed, lifted up Josh's
arm, and crawled underneath. We slept in that morning, alternating
between warm snuggles and wakefulness for the next few hours.

When we finally got up, Josh made us sunny side up eggs and blue-
berry pancakes. I hardly wanted to ruin the perfect breakfast, but I
was a scrambled mix of emotions.

"Joshycito," I started, "I really love you."

"Aw, Lilybillygoat, I love you, too. You are my everything."

"Josh, that's just it," I said sadly, "I don't want you to be my everything."

"Li-ly," he said, pronouncing each syllable very slowly, and with
open arms, gesturing for me to come and sit down on his lap at the
table, still filled with the remnants of our delicious breakfast.

And then, despite my best efforts at holding it in, I vomited my
feelings all over my Josh.

"I need to have a job. And now that I've uprooted myself to be
with you, it needs to be a job that I care about. For me. And babies?
Josh, are we really ready? Am I ready? I mean, I need to have a place
to go where I have to shower and get dressed and put on work appropriate clothing. I need to be outside the house. I, I, I can't just be
home full time with a tiny little screaming, p—p—p—pooping person. Listen to me, I'm already stuttering. I never stuttered before we
moved here. And with a baby, on top of everything else, I'll go completely bonkers. I have moved far away from all of my family and all
of my friends and I am afraid of raising a child here. Will I even be a
good mother? We won't be the same 'us' anymore after a baby. We'll
send holiday cards with pictures of us and our children, smiling and
laughing and playing in our yard. We'll become like every other boring suburban family. What's happening to us?" It all came out like it

was one sentence. Josh held back half a chuckle at my outburst. He motioned again for me to sit down on his lap, and this time, I agreed. "Lily, my love, where is all of this coming from? I love you. You love me. I thought we were doing okay. Is this all about the baby? We talked about this before we got married. I thought you wanted to have kids. I thought we were ready then."

"Josh, we are okay, but you know me, I don't like just okay. I am changing so much, all the time. This place is changing me, and some of that is good, but it's just so much change, so fast, that I don't even know who I am anymore."

I couldn't take the secret letter in my mental filing cabinet another second, "Have I changed too much for you? Is that why you are leaving me and going to Cornell?" I started to cry.

He tapped me on the nose and kissed both cheeks, "Oh Lily, what in the world are you talking about? I am not going to Cornell. Where are you getting this from?" It was clear to me that he hadn't recently checked the filing system I set up for him.

"Josh, I saw the letter. I opened it and read it and put it in your file. Why didn't we talk about this before you sent it off? What if I don't want to move back to the Northeast?" There it was, I was finally getting out some good, honest, communication. I felt temporarily proud of myself.

"Oh Lily, I am not running off anywhere, not without you anyway," he tried to wink at me, but I was having none of it. "This is just the way our department asks us to get our names around, so that when it's time to go up for tenure, our committee knows that we have other offers and it makes us more competitive. I know it doesn't make much sense, but that's the truth. I would never walk out on us. And as far as you changing, well, you have, but that is not totally a bad thing. You, Lily Walker Stone, you lovely creature, are the same fiery, brilliant Lily that I married, you just live in the 'wassee now, so you have had to adapt. We are always going to change, it's just that I hope we can change together."

He smoothed back my hair from my face and cupped the back of my head with both hands, "I probably don't tell you often enough how much I appreciate all the sacrifices you have made to be with me."

I cuddled into his chest. "Is it hard for you, too? You never say."

"I have you, Lily. I have work that moves me. Our families are healthy, and we have many friends who live far away, and we get to talk to them on the phone. Sure, sometimes I wish that I could sit down with a friend, or my brother, and have coffee or a scotch or something, but 99.9% of the time, I feel like the luckiest man on Earth."

"We're both really lucky, Josh. Life with you in the 'wassee is better than life without you anywhere else."

Chapter 19

Rosa

Miami, Florida
October 14, 2006

Querida Diary,

I am sorry that I have not written for a while. I can see that the last time I wrote was when the police came to check on me, and the Cuencas beat me and beat me until I was unconscious. They allowed me to sleep through the night that night, or perhaps they were unable to wake me, bruised and damaged as I was. They did manage to throw me out of my sleeping bag at the usual early time the following morning and force me to cook their breakfast and clean the house. Every part of my body ached. Every step was extremely painful. I moved too slowly for them, and they continued to yell terrible things at me. They didn't hit me anymore that morning, though. I guess they recognized that since Ana was already gone, it might look more suspicious if I died, too. I am embarrassed to say that I thought very much about killing myself that day. I imagined dying Romeo and Juliet style, taking one of the really sharp knives that I used to cut meat and sticking it straight into my side, blood pouring on their nice white carpet.

It did seem like things could not get worse, but they really did. To punish me for showering in the backyard, they decided that morning that they would make sure, for certain, that I didn't leave the house at all, except for Sunday morning. Señora Cuenca got a padlock out and locked the front and back doors from the other sides, so that I would not think it was a good idea again to "shower in the yard like an animal." She told me that "animals are to stay inside the house," and because I was an animal, that is where I would need to stay.

I cried very much that day, the first day that they locked me in the house. I would not give them the satisfaction of crying in front of them, so I held it together, thinking of Ana and Mami and happier times inside my head whenever they were around. After a few days, being locked inside didn't bother me so much. I realized that I was basically locked inside before, and that I still got to go out on Sunday. As much as I hated and feared Martin, he was the one that would drive us to misa on Sundays. He liked the windows down, and I loved the feel of the sun and wind through my hair. I would stick my head out of the car a little and smile into the sun. "Like a stupid dog," Señora Cuenca would say. At those moments, I did feel happy as a dog. Not the stray ones, rib bones poking from tightly stretched skin, that wandered desperately in search for their next meal, but the happy ones from American television that I saw from time to time, gobbling plates of food lovingly given to them straight from their owners' hands.

The moments of freedom in the car extended to time in the church, those wonderfully shiny wooden pews where I got to think about God and Jesus and Mami and Papi and Maria. I loved listening to the music. The hymns reminded me of all that is good in the world. It was usually during those mornings that I renewed my desire to live. I would make a pact with God on those Sunday mornings that I would live to speak with him next week, if he would keep my family safe and keep me strong enough to make it through the week for another talk with him the following Sunday.

This past Sunday, after church, Martin took us home and then ran off with one girlfriend or another, and Señora Cuenca headed to the store to do the shopping for the week. My nightmare began when Señor Cuenca and I were alone together in the house.

"Let's take a shower," he said.

"No thank you, Señor Cuenca."

"Please," he said, "call me Jorge."

"Please Señor Cuenca, I would rather not." I tried to protest, I did. I said no in every way that a good, respectable girl would. Even as he grabbed me and ripped at my nice church clothes, and I pleaded with him not to. He wouldn't listen. He said terrible things into my ear as he stripped me naked and threw me into the shower with him.

"Let me watch you while you clean yourself, you dirty little animal." He seemed to derive great pleasure from this, and I tried to look away as he touched his private place while he watched me. After a few minutes, he closed his eyes, breathed some short, fitful breaths, and then exhaled slowly. He smiled, then, and I watched some thick liquid drip down his leg.

"You are a sexy little animal," he said to me, grabbing at my body. I was too scared to soap down and actually clean myself. He was in the process of cleaning himself off when I heard Señora Cuenca's car come into the driveway. I panicked and tried to quickly get clean. Señor Cuenca clearly didn't hear the car over the noise of the shower and he was in no hurry to get going. He grabbed at my body from every direction, making noises that sounded like half happiness, and half pain. A few moments later, Señora Cuenca came into the bathroom, thinking that her husband was alone in there. The shower had steamed a good bit, but not enough to cover up the fact that there was another body in the shower with him.

"*Que en el demonio esta pasando aqui?*" Señora Cuenca furiously demanded to know what was going on in the shower. She slid open the shower door with all her force and found me in there with Señora Cuenca. She stood for a second, shocked, just letting the water pour out of the shower and flood the floor. Señor Cuenca slid out the other side of the shower, and I just stood there, naked, embarrassed, and without a clue as to what to do next.

"Shut off the shower, you stupid slut," she barked at me. When I didn't respond fast enough, she reached in herself to shut off the water, dampening her nice church clothes. She was too angry to notice.

"How dare you? … in my own home? … after all we have done for you? You try to seduce my husband? Who do you think you are?" She had pulled me out of the shower by this point, and had a tight grip around my throat, pushing me back into the counter where they kept their toothbrushes and paste, perfumes and razors.

I tried to protest, to tell her that it was not my idea to take a shower with her husband, that it wasn't what she thought, but she would not hear a single word of it.

"How dare you do this to me … in my own home!?" As she spat those words in my face, she twisted my right arm so hard around my back that I shrieked out in pain. She kept twisting it and twisting it, asking me that same question over and over again without permitting me to respond.

Eventually, my arm made a snapping sound. *Señora* Cuenca let go, and I fell to the ground, holding my twisted arm with my other good one.

"If I ever see you messing around with my husband again, I will break your other arm, you stupid slut. Now get out of my bathroom."

It was hard to get up, Diary. My arm hurt so much, but I needed to get out of the room. I walked out of the room as fast as I possibly could, and caught a sidelong glance of Señor Cuenca as I did. Confident that Señora Cuenca could not see him from that angle, he looked at me and put his lips together in a silent kissing motion. I felt dizzy and sick, both from the pain, and the embarrassment of all that I had been accused of.

Why were all of these terrible things happening to me? I wanted to wake up and find myself back in Jujuy, but I thought then that it would never happen, that the Cuencas would kill me or worse, hurt Maria or Mami if I ever told on them.

I wasn't sure that I would be able to keep my promise with God this week. It was only Sunday afternoon, and there was a whole week to endure before Sunday came around again.

Until then,

Rosa

Chapter 20

Mila

Working at the VIP became less fun than it was that first night, when I had actually thought that I would get some performance experience. Sure, I am still performing, in fact, my current work requires a great deal of acting. Although I am learning how to be a dancer in the nude entertainment industry, much of my "performance" work is now done in private.

I don't dare tell Chico about this work, but my nightly tips have tripled and I bet he must suspect what I am up to each night. I wish I could keep more of the money I earn for myself, but I still have to hand over 25% to Sebastian. After that, I hand the rest over to Chico when he picks me up. It's no big deal, really, because whenever I want something, Chico either buys it for me, or takes me with him and buys it. I don't want for anything, really.

Every other night at work is basically the same, except Monday. My favorite night of the week now is Monday night, the only night when I don't have to work at the VIP I drive home from Hunan with Chico and Jose and make them dinner. I have learned how to make all of their favorites: rice and beans, plantains, mojo chicken. They love my cooking. After I cook, we eat, drink beers and laugh. Chico tells me that drinking beer like they do, straight from a bottle or can is not something that a lady would do, and instead, he gets me whatever wine or cocktail I want. I started drinking mixed drinks at the club. You know, the sex on the beach, or a sea breeze. I especially love to order the cosmopolitan. I liked to pretend I am Samantha, the older, sexy blonde from the American television show Sex and the City. I swirl the straw in my drink around with my tongue and lure in the men for the evening. I don't even need to mix in the fruit juice or the sodas now to my alcohol, and anyway, I don't need the calories. My body makes me a lot of money and I need to stay thin to keep bringing in the cash.

I love the feel of cold crisp vodka as it slides down my throat. After

I clear the table and finish the dishes, I grab Chico's hand and the bottle of vodka and we get into bed. He likes for me to show him how I dance for the customers and then we make love, usually twice. I drink more now than I used to, and I know that I shouldn't. It's just hard. It's hard to be so conscious of everything that the men want to do to me at work, and sometimes with Chico, especially when he gets a little rough with me, it feels more like work than play, except he doesn't give me any money for my time with him. I love Chico, but lately it feels better loving him when I've had a few drinks first. Things feel different between us now and I don't know why.

"Hey Mila," he said to me one night, roughly reaching over my naked body, to get to the vodka. "I really wish you were making more money. I feel like Jose and I are shouldering so much responsibility at work, and it makes me so tense."

I was exhausted, and pretty drunk. Although I had built up quite a tolerance over the past few months, I had probably had half the bottle of vodka since I got home from work, and barely ate all day. I nodded sympathetically. I didn't really know what else to say to Chico at that point. I was already working two full jobs and I couldn't remember ever feeling so tired.

"Mila, it would be great if you would spend some time being nice to Jose, too," he said, gesturing through the partially open door toward Jose in the kitchen. He is very lonely.

Although I was tired, I tried to suppress the anger rising up inside of me. Jose? He had tried to rape me. I hated Jose. Still, if it would make Chico happy if I were nicer to his brother, then so be it, I would swallow my disappearing pride and be nicer to Jose.

"Of course, my love, I will be nice to your brother."

"I'm so glad, Mila, I mean, after all that we do for you, it would be a nice way to show that you appreciate us." With that, Chico snapped his fingers and called loudly to his brother. "*Oye, Papi, Mila esta lista.*" I didn't know it at the time, but Chico was telling my brother that I was ready for him.

I could see Jose from the slightly ajar door. I saw him spit on his greasy hands and rub them through his greasy hair. Chico got up, put on some clothes and left the room. He left me there with Jose. I had had too much to drink, sure, but I knew that I didn't want to be alone

– again – with Jose. I didn't trust him. I tried to be nice to him, like Chico said.

"Hi Jose, did you have enough to eat? Did you want me to cook you something else?" As I nervously talked, and tried to cover myself up with the covers, Jose walked over to the bed and began to pin me down with his hands.

"Sorry, Mila, I'm still hungry for something else." He kissed me all over my neck and I pleaded with him to stop. He didn't. I called Chico's name once. He didn't answer. I tried calling louder, but I could hear Chico turning up the radio in the living room to a volume loud enough to drown out my voice. He turned it up so loud that I hoped that our neighbors would complain about the noise and that someone would peel Jose off me. I called for Chico and tried to push Jose off. It was no use.

Jose had sex with me that night, and after he was done, and left the room, I crawled into the shower and sat in the tub for a long time, just letting the water wash over me. How could Chico have let that happen? I didn't understand how he could do that to me.

Chico must have left while I was in the shower because he never came back to our bed that night, and in the morning he still wasn't there. Jose gave me a lift to work. We didn't say much of anything to each other in the car, at least he left me alone that much. I wandered through the next day in a half-haze. I don't remember much, other than my head hurt, and I had pain in my abdomen where Jose had been rough with me. Mainly, I felt used, and I had a large pain in my heart that Chico would have let his brother be with me like that. I vowed to talk to him at the end of the long day, after work at the VIP.

Katie and Britney noticed that I seemed a bit off, and they asked if I was okay. I tried to let them know that I was, but they assumed it was the work at the VIP that was getting to me.

Britney sat me down at one point, while we were serving drinks and said, "Baby, you know that I know that this life can be hard. But look at you! You are so gosh darn beautiful, and all the men here just love you. You are making so much money, you are going to be out of here in no time, I just know it."

I loved her southern accent, like Julia Roberts in *Steel Magnolias*.

She had a smile that lit something inside me, made me feel loved. Her voice, and the gentle squeeze she gave me around the shoulders was really comforting.

"I just don't know if I can continue on like this, Brit. I am tired. Really tired." I felt more exhausted at that moment than I ever had before.

"I know you are tired, baby, so am I. It's been a long night. It's been many long nights. But it won't go on forever like this. I have a plan."

Britney spent the next while talking my ear off about how she wants to go to Florida, where the really rich men live, not these small timers at the VIP in Atlanta. She plans to land a nice, rich old man and then just lay back, drink "some nice bourbon and soak in the rays and seashore." Just as soon as she can, Britney is "out of this dump."

"Oh darling, I don't mean to call it a dump. It's certainly a livin', but it's not a way to live, you know? I wanted better for myself. Tell you what? It sure would be fun if you would come with me, too. What do you say, darling? Come to Florida with me! We will have such a blast, meetin' men and swimmin' in the ocean."

Britney was so excited I wanted to jump in that Florida ocean along with her, but it was her dream, not mine. I already had a great man in my life who took good care of me. At least I thought I did. I couldn't believe what had happened the night before. Did I remember it wrong? I can't imagine that Chico would have known that Jose would try to have sex with me and then just let it happen. Jose is his brother, but Chico seems too proud for that. I was anxious to speak with him about it after work.

He was always there like clockwork, right on time at 2 a.m., waiting for me. The other girls were always jealous when they saw Chico, coming out to open my car door with his big, strong arms and tight pants that showed off his manhood. It was already 2:15 in the morning, though, and he wasn't there. Britney waited with me, afraid that I might stand outside alone, where the air was still a chilly, and sometimes the customers waited outside, too, to see if they could grab something for free. We waited. And waited.

"Babylove, I am so sorry to do this to you, but the last bus is at 3:30 a.m. and I have to take it or I won't ever get back home. You going to be okay without me? I'm sure he'll come. Why don't you try texting him again. Here, you know his number, right? You can use my phone."

And just then, Chico drove up. I was so relieved to see him. I said a quick goodbye to Brit, thanking her for staying as long as she did, and hopped into the car. When I did, Chico seemed distant, and I could smell beer on his breath.

"Oh my Chico, where were you? I was starting to worry." As I talked to Chico, I ran my hands over his body and leaned in to kiss him on the cheek.

He intercepted my kiss, and while driving, reached his left hand over his right and slapped me on the face.

"Don't touch me until you have showered. I don't want to catch some disease from you." He looked at me with disgust. I didn't understand. What was going on? Did I do something wrong? Why would I have a disease?

He couldn't really mean it. "Chico" I said, as I gently squeezed his thigh. He grabbed my hand on his thigh and twisted it hard over my head as he continued to drive, recklessly, toward the apartment.

"I mean it, Mila" he growled at me, "don't touch me until you have cleaned yourself."

I winced in pain and he let my arm go. Why was Chico treating me like this? Hadn't I done everything he wanted? Maybe this had to do with Jose. Maybe Jose, that little jerk, had filled his head with lies about me.

We got home, parked the car, and I trailed after Chico, all the way up the stairs toward the apartment. I didn't try to talk to him anymore, because I could see it would be no use.

I went straight into the shower, not wanting to anger Chico again. I sat down in the steaming water and cried. What kind of mess had I got myself into? Should I just go home to Bratislava? Ugh, I couldn't. I didn't work so hard just to turn around and go back without ever trying to make it as an actress at all. I just couldn't. I would stay. I would pay off my debt and sock away some money, and then Chico and I would head to New York. He would change back to the Chico he had been before, I just knew it. He was just stressed about the money, and I would take care of that.

I came out of the shower, and was rubbing my hair dry with a small blue towel. I walked into the pitch black room I shared with Chico.

"Chico, I'm here now, and I'm completely clean from the shower." No answer.

"Chico?" I said, to the lump of a body in our bed. He sat up, he had no shirt on, and it was not Chico.

"Jose! Chico is not going to want you in our bed, please go back to your room at once!"

Jose laughed at me from the bed, and I heard Chico laughing as he entered the room.

"Oh Mila, you think you can just save it for the boys at the club and not give any to Jose and me." His voice had a horrible tone: half mocking, entirely mean.

"Chico, stop, please. I have never held back from you. I love you." I pleaded. It was heartfelt, but I must have sounded pathetic to them.

"Oh yeah? You love me, Mila." He laughed again. "Well, I am a Latin man, and we are very close to our families. Loving me means loving my whole family. Tonight, it's Jose's turn for you to love him."

I started to cry. "Please, no, Chico. No no no no no no no. Don't do this to me."

Chico threw me down on the bed. He was big and strong and I had no way to fight him off.

"We can't have you giving it away all night at the club and leaving nothing for *la familia*. Enjoy her, big brother, and when you are done, give me a yell and I'll come in."

Just like that, he was gone. I knew, that instant, that this was not a good kind of love. I knew that Chico must have heard Jose with me the night before, and that it was no accident. Sex with Jose was horrible. He kept covering my mouth to keep me from screaming, and he scratched and clawed at me like a beast. The only good thing was that he did agree to wear a condom, but only because he said that he wanted to protect himself from my diseases. It felt like forever, but it was over pretty quickly according to the clock. Jose left the room and called for Chico.

He came in, crawled into bed where Jose had lain, and stroked my hair. I turned away from him on my side and pretended to be asleep.

"I love you, Mila," he said, gently into my ear. "Thank you for doing that for my brother. He is a good guy and he needed you, just like I need you."

I didn't know what to say, so I stayed quiet, let him put his large arm around my waist, and tried to keep my breathing measured, in and out, in and out. Eventually I fell asleep.

Chapter 21

Lily

I've got some ideas about how to keep my operation going, and I am running with them. I have been speaking to various community organizations and trying to spread the word about the needs of immigrant women in this part of the state. People have been shocked, and surprisingly receptive. I am endlessly amused by the initial "What????" that I receive when I talk about the various ways that immigrants are exploited right here in the Florida Panhandle.[46]

"What? Can't be. Not here in Hiawassee Springs." I swear it should be the official city slogan. You have to admire that level of disbelief. I understood their shock, given that this a place where people do take care of each other. I wanted to believe that it wasn't possible right along with them, but I knew all too well what could happen here. I had seen the worn faces of the people who were slipping through the cracks of an otherwise caring and tightly knit community.

Last month I spoke to Zonta, Rotary, and other groups of local businessmen and women. I only have to share pieces of the stories of my clients for people to pull out their wallets and checkbooks and say, "How much?" When I speak to church groups, and other people with very limited funds they say, "What can I do? How can I help?" I have already received so many donations at work that I have had to dedicate a portion of my already closet-like office for food and toy donations. I hadn't anticipated this level of commitment. Maybe I had seen too much Lou Dobbs, but I anticipated more anti-immigrant sentiment than I have found. Certainly, some people have voiced concern that "these people" have brought the situation on themselves by coming to the country illegally. I actually had one couple complain

---

46. Although, it was hard to tell whether the disbelief was because immigrants lived among us or because these immigrants were being exploited. Either way, folks seemed surprised and upset.

to me that all the "Mexicans" in their neighborhood reeked of urine and should be forced to go back to their own country, where such a stench was permitted. It was my turn to say, "What??????" Still, the vast majority of the people I have met want to keep the IJC afloat to help our vulnerable clients.

Speaking to various groups in my quest for donations has had many positive effects. Probably not the most important, but perhaps one of the most entertaining has been my exposure to Panhandle style. I have really loved some of the hairdos and shades of pink that I have observed throughout my crazy whistle-stop tour through this part of Florida. Now, I have never been the most fashionable in my cohort, even when I was making the big bucks at the law firm. But seriously, folks around these parts are frozen in the 1980s. We've got big hair, those big glasses for men, lots of shoulder pads, colorful pumps, and hair-sprayed bangs. I almost expect to hear "Billy Jean" booming from a huge stereo slung across someone's shoulders wherever I go. I love their big hair and their big hearts. I never knew it was possible, but for all its ups and downs, I also love the 'wassee.

Despite the popular fashions, time moves forward, and in the present, I remain desperate to fund continuous care and services to battered and abused immigrant women in North Florida. Because I have not told anyone that I might not be able to continue doing my job, the clients keep coming, and I just can't bring myself to turn them away, especially when I know there is nowhere else for them to go for immigration assistance within a few hundred mile radius.

Just yesterday, in fact, I had a new client come to my office, Adriana Gonzalez. Adriana entered the U.S. illegally from Mexico seven years earlier, bringing three of her children with her, and leaving the youngest daughter behind with Adriana's mother. *Pobrecita*, Adriana. Her boyfriend Vicente, the father of three of the children, was terribly abusive. He called her "fat" and "stupid" and he hit her on the face and arms, all in front of the children. At age 13, the oldest son, Ignacio, or "Nacho" for short, started to take after his father. He said terrible things to Adriana, who had two jobs cleaning hotel rooms and private homes to make ends meet. One day, when Vicente was working a night shift and little Nacho got mad that his mother wouldn't let him play video games, he kicked her in the abdomen. When she collapsed in pain, lying prostrate on the ground, he kicked at her sides, legs and back, until Adriana had to call out to her nine-year-old daughter Teresa, scared and whimpering in the corner, to call 9-1-1. Teresa called, and the police came, and they took Nacho to a rehabilitative program for troubled teens, and Adriana's boyfriend got mad at her for involving the police, so he beat her more. She showed up at my office with a bruised and swollen half-open eye.

I knew that Adriana was eligible for legal relief, but we had a question to resolve: would she name both her boyfriend and her son on the petition, exposing them both to potential deportation? She depended on her boyfriend financially, and she loved Nacho, despite his problems. It was not a matter to resolve in one day. After a few hours, and fistfuls of tissues, she left my office. I knew that she had only two places to go: back home, or to the police station. Adriana still had two other children at home to look after. I don't pray often, but I did after we met, that Vicente would leave Adriana and those children alone, at least until we could find her a safer place to live.

Each week I hear a story like Adriana's. Each and every day I meet someone whose needs seem more immediate, and more dire than the last. Some of the women I am representing have absolutely nowhere to go, and they sleep in their cars. One of them had an urgent dental problem, and described the daily pain as "making childbirth feel like a big nothing." So, in addition to free legal services, my clients certainly have much more crucial needs. What these folks really need is a safe place to stay, one where they can get all the medical, dental, mental and other health care that they require. Homeless shelters are good for temporary emergencies, but when you have come to this country, you don't speak the language, and you have been abused or abandoned (or both), you need all kinds of assistance that a homeless shelter can't give. I figured that I could just kill two birds with one stone and start a program at the homeless shelter, or depending on how much money I could get, maybe even a separate shelter for immigrant victims of domestic violence who have no place to go. I don't know the first thing about building a shelter, but this is a community that cares, and I knew they would want to help me do something.

The days are long, but I hardly notice. I have basically been working seven days a week, sunup to sundown. I rarely take the time to eat, and recently became wary of any food item not wrapped in a foil wrapper. I have continued that schedule: wake, work at IJC, speak to local groups after work, collapse, sleep, repeat, for several months now. I knew that I was tired, and that I was probably neglecting Josh, but he didn't complain, and I was too tired to really care. I was probably suffering from a bit of compassion fatigue, where everyone else's problems paled in comparison to those of my clients. I could no longer listen to my old friend's complaints about her pursuit of the perfect shoes without wanting to hang up on her, and then smash the phone against the wall repeatedly, pretending it was her head. Okay, maybe the problem was just fatigue, sans compassion.

One Thursday, around midnight, when I finally got home, crawled into bed and collapsed, Josh tried to speak with me, and wasn't entirely satisfied by my grunts-as-responses.

"Lilybillygoat, I really need to talk."

"HrRRfer," I replied, and I meant it. These days I could have slept through a nuclear meltdown and thought I was just dreaming that cockroaches had been the sole survivors of the war.

"Lilybug," he said, as he gently touched my face, hoping the sensation of being prodded about the face would work. It didn't.

"Lily!" I had done it. I had finally exasperated the kindest, gentlest, most patient man known to, well, man. "I can't take it anymore. Do you even notice that I'm here?"

"Josh, why are you yelling?" I took one of the spare pillows on our bed, pressed it over my head, and tried to get back to sleep.

"Lily, I am proud of you, I really am. I want you to be happy here, and I am thrilled that you have found a job that you really care about, but, but ..."

I tried to gently ask, "But what, Josh?" It was hard for me not to just go crazy on him. Josh hated ever to hurt anyone's feelings. He hated conflict almost as much as he hated to hurt people. The only problem was that when he finally did uncork the frustration bottle, it exploded all over the place.

"But I am your husband and I need your love!" he shouted at me, even though our faces were only inches apart while we lay on the same bed.[47]

I tried with everything I had not to laugh at him. It's not something I am proud of, but it's definitely a flaw. As a child, I never got into trouble at school, except for the two times (once in second grade, and once in eleventh) where I descended into uncontrollable laughter and the teachers forced me to leave the classroom and to return only when I could control myself. I fought back the laughter, but I felt the corners of my mouth turning into a smile-smirk, and I knew things were going straight downhill. I lost it.

Josh stared back at me in stunned silence. He had never seen my laughter hysterics, nor had he heard the stories. He looked at me with utter disappointment for a moment or two, but then he, too, was drawn in by the intoxicating power of the Lilylaugh (as they used to call it), and we laughed until we could barely breathe and it hurt. Sometime after the laughter eventually died down, we both felt heaps better. I felt a reprieve from some of the work-related stress and exhaustion, and Josh felt like he had been heard. We made love that night, and for the first time, somewhere within me I hoped that in our consensus over laughter, we may have also created life.

---

47. We had purchased a double bed, which I refer to as a "mandatory cuddling" number as opposed to the larger king-sized version which permits "discretionary cuddling." I figured, who needs all that discretion in the beginning of a marriage, right? Turns out we probably did, and more often than I'd really like to admit. It took so long to find the right guy, and I had moved far away from everyone and everything that I knew to be with him, and now what? I couldn't very well just walk out on him. He deserved better than that and so did I. We had promised to stick it out, for better or worse.

Chapter 22

Rosa

Miami, Florida
December 8, 2006

Querida Diary,

The days have been dark for me. The sun must rise and set, but I only see daylight on Sundays: for that, I believe in God. He gives me light one day each week. My arm still hurts where Señora Cuenca twisted it, especially on days when it rains. I wake each morning, thinking of Ana, wondering if I would be better off being with her somewhere beyond this world. I know I can't take much more of this.

Once a week, I feel human again. The other days and nights pass without much difference between them. The Cuencas continue to be very cruel, especially Señora Cuenca, who sometimes locks me in my room at night. "So you won't go after my husband again." I don't know how she can really believe that that is what happened. I try my best not to drink too much water in the evenings so that I won't have to leave my room to use the bathroom. That only happened once, and my need to go was so profound that I wet myself instead. I told Señora Cuenca and she refused to give me another sleeping bag, or to let me buy another change of clothes. I smelled of urine for days, and I finally felt like the animal they kept telling me I was.

It is Sunday, though, and on Sundays life gets a little better. There is the promise of something different, and those blissful hours when I get to sit in the church, and hear the music, and feel like I am just as

125

good in God's eyes as any one of the other people in the pews. On Sundays, I don't feel like God has forgotten me.

There is a boy that I have seen in church. He smiles at me from across the aisle, and he has tried to talk to me many times. Anytime the Cuencas see us about to talk, they yank me away. Still, he has the nicest face. His name is Marco. English is his second language, so we can talk together in Spanish. He is nice. He brings me candy sometimes, and always tells me that I look pretty. Last week the Cuencas tried to pull me away, but Marco started talking to them, and they didn't want to be rude to him. It turns out that he is Colombian, like Señora Cuenca, and they are even from towns very near to each other, and the Cuencas know one of Marco's cousins.

This particular Sunday, the Cuencas greeted Marco and then gave us more time alone to talk. I think the cousin in common keeps them from wanting to show Marco any disrespect. Also, he is almost 18 years old, so he is more like an adult.

"Te invito a una fiesta, Rosa," Come to a party with me, Rosa, Marco asked, seemingly out of nowhere. "It is at my cousin Juan's house. There will be music and dancing. What do you say? You'll come, yes?"

His smile could have lit up even the darkest street in Jujuy. I wanted very badly to go to his party with him.

"I have to ask the Cuencas," I explained, as if he couldn't already tell, that I didn't come and go as I pleased. Still, I was intoxicated by the church, heady with all the freedom and beauty that comes just once a week.

"You shouldn't have to ask. I'm the man. I will. Dulce Rosita, let me do this properly." I watched him stride proudly toward the Cuencas, and they spoke with intensity for several minutes. Marco stepped away and walked toward the bathroom.

Diary, I then walked over to the Cuencas and proceeded to ask Señora Cuenca whether I could go to the party with Marco for just a few hours. She seemed shocked at first, that I would be so bold, but her face muscles relaxed, her jaw unclenched as she realized that she did not want Marco to have a bad impression of her or of our relationship.

"It is fine for you to spend time with Marco, Rosa, just make sure you are back to the house by 9 p.m. and that your work does not suffer for it."

I could have hugged her. Well, I couldn't have brought myself to actually hug her, after all that she had put me through, and I still could not lift my right arm above my shoulder, but still, I briefly felt real happiness and kindness towards her. I had a moment of self-realization where I was surprised and warmed that I could actually feel something so nice again. I thought I really must be taking in the teachings of Jesus if I could feel love for Señora Cuenca.

I walked back over to Marco who had filled a plastic cup with red fizzy fruit punch for me with chunks of green sorbet floating around. I smiled and thanked him as I took a small sip from the cup.

"Yes, Marco, me voy contigo a la fiesta." I told Marco I would go to the party with him. I felt full of excitement. I felt free.

We walked out to his white pickup truck and he opened the passenger car door for me. I blushed. We drove for the next 10 minutes or so back to his house.

"I just need to run inside and pick up my wallet. I accidentally left it home. Do you want to wait in the truck or inside? It may take me a minute to find it."

I felt myself getting very tired. Maybe I was coming down with a cold, or maybe it was because I had barely had anything to eat all day.

"If you don't mind, Marco, I think I'll just stay here while you get your wallet."

"Okay, Rosa." He winked at me, flashed that beautiful smile, and touched my hand. My eyes filled with tears. I hadn't had someone touch me with so much kindness in such a long, long time. I felt the tears slide down my cheeks, and I felt too tired to bother to wipe them away. I let the wetness collect at the base of my neck, on my blouse, darkening my lace collar on the one nice dress I had brought with me.

Diary, I tell you that I remember little else of what happened next, but when I woke, I was in a bed, there was blood on the sheets, and in my underwear. Where were my clothes? It was light outside and the clock was flashing 12:00 a.m. I started to scream.

Marco came in a few seconds later and forced a hand over my mouth. He held it there while he explained the situation. He told me that we never ended up going to the party because I had fallen asleep in the car, and he took me inside his house and put me in the bed. Marco told me that he had bought me from the Cuencas, that I was his now, and that I would do as he said. That beautiful white smile seemed sinister to me now. I felt impossibly tired, like I could sleep and sleep and sleep for days.

While I slept I dreamt of Ana. Always Ana. I dreamt that we were on an adventure, walking through waterfalls, laughing as the water danced down upon our heads. When I woke again it was not a waterfall, but Marco, he threw some water at my face.

"Despiertate, you lazy girl," Wake up, he said, his voice devoid of any kindness.

He told me that I had been sleeping for thirteen hours. For a brief minute I had forgotten about what he told me before. I quickly realized, despite the drowsy cloud I was fighting off, that I was naked, and that he was looking at me inappropriately. I didn't want to be there with him, but where would I go? I certainly didn't want to go back to the Cuencas. I wanted to go home. But like this? Naked in a strange man's bed? I am a virgin. Or at least, I was a virgin. Oh God, what happened? How could I ever face Mami again? I tried to cover myself up with the blood stained sheet. I began to cry. Marco slapped me clean across the face.

He ripped the covers away from me so hard that it burned the skin on my inner thigh as I held onto the sheets. "Oh, now you are trying to cover up? After you begged me to fuck you? You are a dirty little whore. Don't even think about going back to the Cuencas. I bought you fair and square, and you weren't cheap. I bought your debt, Rosita, and you'll pay me back. You'll pay back every centavo!" He grabbed at my breast as he said this, and I recoiled.

"You will not refuse me, just like you didn't refuse me last night. You need to work off your debt. I know people who would like a young thing like you. You will be with them, and you will hand the money over to me. When you are done, and your debt is paid, you are free to go."

The tears kept coming to my eyes. I was scared and humiliated. I wanted Mami.

Diary, I cannot bear to write down all the things that Marco did to me. He was even more cruel that the Cuencas, if that is possible. The Cuencas worked all day, so I had time alone to do the chores, cooking and cleaning. I was lonely there, but at least I had time to myself. Marco was recently out of a job, so he had all day long to take out his anger and disappointment on me. He made me work all night, every night. He would drive me – and he made me crouch down in the car to be sure that no one saw me with him in the car – to a few different mobile homes where he arranged for many men, sometimes 10 or 15 each night, to have their way with me. I begged him to tell these men to wear condoms so that I would not have to bear the child of one of them. He finally agreed.

I would spend my nights having sex with strange men for money. I don't know how to describe how very terrible it was. Marco didn't let me sleep much, and I felt too tired to move most of the time. He made sure that he was the last man to take me each night, and the first each morning, and he told me that that made me his. It made me hurt so much in my private area. Sometimes it hurt to pee. During the day I would cook and clean for Marco, and he was sometimes nice then. Other times, he would pull my hair really hard and hit me for no reason at all. At least at the Cuencas I was allowed to go to church with them on Sundays. Marco said that I was a "puta" and that he couldn't trust me even at church not to be looking at other men. He felt like the only way I could stay his was if I never left his sight in the apartment. A whole year of my life passed, and the only time I saw the outside world was through the eyes of the men who hurt me.

I don't feel like writing any more now. I hope you can understand.

Love,

Rosa

Chapter 23

Mila

I woke up the day after Chico made me have sex with his brother feeling worse than ever. How could Chico do that to me? I had never felt so betrayed. I looked over and saw that he had left a note for me, with a pink rose, my favorite.

"I love you, Mila. Thank you. Love, Chico." It was a small gesture, but for my strong macho man, it was a big deal. I knew that Chico loved me. I felt better, for the time being. I showered and dressed for work. Jose and I drove over to Hunan together, his hand resting on my thigh. I threw it off again and again, but he would laugh his sinister stupid laugh and put it right back on the middle of my thigh.

"Really, Mila, you are still fighting me off? I will take you tonight just like I did last night, and you won't be able to brush me away." He leaned over, put his disgusting mouth near my ear and exhaled deeply, licking the inside.

I could not have arrived at work a moment sooner. As I entered in the back, a few employees were already there chopping vegetables.

"Hey Kat," I said, with as much enthusiasm as I had at the time, which wasn't much. She had headphones on and nodded in my direction. We were not about to become best friends like Rachel and Monica living in New York City and sharing an apartment anytime soon. I caught Chico's eye through a window and he gave me a wink. I felt better, just seeing his face.

The day passed quickly, and I went to take a 5 minute bathroom break. I rounded the corner and noticed that the hall closet door was locked, and some noises were coming from the room. I checked the clock on the wall and knew I had only 2 minutes left of my regulated break, and that if I took any longer one of the other employees may well have told on me, like one of the double crossers in an Indiana Jones movie. Still, I was worried about what was going on in the closet and I suspected the worst, so I decided to wait it out. I saw the doorknob jiggle and I had nowhere to hide. I was still standing there when Chico emerged from the space that we had shared several times a week. He was sweaty, red in the face, and still doing up his zipper when he saw me. Kat followed behind him, avoided my eyes, ducked under his large, muscled arm, and headed through the door and back to work.

"Mila," he said, without a hint of apology in his voice.

The room swirled. "How could—" I begin, but he clamped a hand over my mouth.

"Mila, you know I love you, but I have needs that you can't always fulfill. Sometimes you are with Jose, sometimes you are with your clients at the VIP. What am I supposed to do then?"

I didn't have a second to react properly. I felt humiliated, angry, sad, and horrible. "But Chico, I am here now. That closet is our spot." Even then I didn't like how pathetic I sounded to myself. I am Mila Gulej, future actress. What was I even doing here, with this cheating man? Marek may not have been as interesting or sexy as Chico, but he never would have cheated on me.

Chico grabbed me in a large hug, trying to make it all go away. "Shhhh, Mila," he said as he held my body from behind and I sobbed in frustration. "One day you will pay off all your debt to me, and we will go to New York City together, and you will be the famous actress you have always wanted to be."

I nodded through my tears, wanting to believe he meant what he said. It seemed harder to believe now. All I could see was that careless look on his sweaty face as he zipped up his pants, and the lack of remorse when his eyes caught mine.

I passed the rest of the day in a semi-haze, choosing to focus instead on mopping the floor so that I wouldn't have to look directly at Kat: I couldn't help but hate her.

That night at the VIP could not have come quickly enough. From the moment I walked through the door, Britney could tell that something was wrong.

"Hey love, what's going on with you?" She questioned me gently as we sat in the back room, putting on makeup and fishnet stockings. I was glad to escape myself that night and to pretend to be someone else, someone who wasn't stupid enough to be with a cheating boyfriend.

"It's nothing, Britney, just had a long day at work. How are you doing?" I gave it my best performance, but it lacked spirit.

"Oh darlin', I can tell something is wrong. What is it? Can I help?" She sat down next to me, smoothed down my long blonde hair, and gave my slender arm a gentle squeeze. Before she even could let me respond, she tried, "Don't worry, Mila, you and I will be out of this life soon. We're too pretty to work. You and Chico will get married and you'll move to New York, and I'll find me a bizillionaire in Florida and I'll sip fruity drinks all day long. So tell me, sweetie, what's got you so down?"

I just couldn't tell her the truth. Telling Britney what was really going on would have meant that I also would need to come clean to myself, and I had just applied some fresh mascara, and customers would start arriving any minute.

"I'm fine, really. Thanks for caring." I gave her a hug and a smile. I pretended like I was that chubby black haired woman on Designing Women, and tried my best to seem like all I had was a hard day at the office because I ate too much dessert and I was frustrated with my lack of willpower. Britney barely seemed to be buying it, but it was almost midnight, and it was our turn to head out to the stage.

Whatever enjoyment I first got from performing for these American men had long since passed. The only way for me to get through the night was sharing drinks with them and pretending to be somewhere and someone else. Escaping was just what I needed that night. As I danced on stage in panties and swung around a few poles, my thoughts turned to Mother. She always wanted what was best for me, wanted me to be happy. She wouldn't have wanted this.

I wanted so badly to leave, to head to the Big Apple and become a star, but what about my debt? I owed Chico more money than I could pay off anytime soon. But didn't he owe me something, too? I thought he loved me. How could he go and have sex with Kat? I felt myself cooking into a rage. It had taken a lot to get this angry, first with taking on this stupid job to pay off my debt to Chico, then dealing with the humiliation of being forced to be with Jose, then watching Chico come out of our closet (our closet!) with Kat. Something inside me just exploded while I was on stage. It had been a slow boil, but I was now fully cooked. I wanted out. Now!

Our shift ended and I slipped out of my sexy clothes and into something to keep me warm for the chilly fall night. I changed slowly, waiting for the other girls to leave and for Britney and I to have a chance to be alone. Once they were gone, I pounced on my chance.

With blood still raging in my head, I put it out there, "Britney, let's do it." I looked into her eyes, and told her we had to go.

She was unfazed, my urgency didn't register. "Do what, sugar?" she asked, absentmindedly twirling a strand of her curly, strawberry blonde hair as she wiped off her lipstick.

I placed both hands on her shoulders and squared them. "Britney, you have a car and I can't take this one more second. What is keeping you here? It can't be this job. We're better than this. Let's go. I only have twenty minutes before Chico comes to pick me up. I don't want to see him. Please, let's just get in your car and go." I didn't have the heart to tell her that I owed him a lot of money. I didn't know how much really, but whenever I asked Chico he would just say, "Keep working, Mila, and you will pay it all off," but he kept track of all the money, and I probably owe him thousands.

"Oh Mila, sweetie, Chico will come around. Is it another girl? And anyway, it's not my way to make such hasty decisions. I can't even decide what color lipstick to wear in the morning." She waved me away with a laugh. I was desperate. I took her purse and grabbed her keys.

"Britney, I am going with or without you." I grabbed my clothes and her purse, and I was flying out the back exit. Britney, too stunned to respond, just ran after me, and dizzy from confusion, she hopped in the passenger seat.

I tried to start the car and the engine stalled. One hitch to this sudden escape plan of mine: I didn't know how to drive.

"Change of plans, Brit, you drive," I pulled out the keys and tossed them to her. To my surprise, she did as I said. "Hurry, hurry!" I had to get out of there. I couldn't stand it another second.

I slid over to the passenger seat and she took off toward the great unknown, toward anywhere else but here. It all felt very Thelma and Louise. We drove south for several hours before I began to breathe out. The sky was dark and the roads were empty save for a few truck drivers. It was the start of something else.

I turned to Britney. "Brit, we are going to be better off, wherever we are going. I really appreciate this, you know." I smiled at her and squeezed her right shoulder. She turned quickly, wary to take her eyes off the unpaved back road and flashed me a good sized grin.

"Where to now, Miss Bossy Mila?" She asked, a mix of humor and fear in her voice.

Truth was, I had no idea. Still, I could tell that Britney would go along with whatever I came up with as long as I made it sound convincing. I was scared, too, but I couldn't let her know.

"I'm tired, Brit, and we're almost out of gas. How about if we find a motel and get a little sleep. When we wake up, we can figure out what our next move will be."

She agreed, and a few minutes later we passed the "Welcome to Florida, the Sunshine State" sign. We let out a collective "Woohooo!"

Florida, this was where Britney wanted her dreams to come true. We turned off a few miles from that sign at the next exit. We found a Happy Camper Motel and used our cash tips from the night to rent a room. I didn't have any identification (since Chico kept all my documents for safe keeping), and I didn't want Britney to leave a trail of ID in case Chico and Jose came looking for us.

We dragged our things upstairs to Room 209, and each collapsed onto a separate single bed. It was already almost light outside and between my nerves, fear and excitement, I couldn't possibly have slept. Truth was, I had no idea what we would do next. Britney immediately fell asleep while I fretted over our next move. Poor Britney, I felt sorry for dragging her into my mess. I must have dozed off, because the clock said 10:45 a.m. when I woke to the sound of a knock at the door. I froze.

The knocking came again, more insistent. "*Opain up!*" I heard a man's voice with a Spanish sounding accent. I knew it wasn't Chico, but it sounded a lot like him.

Britney sleepily got up and went to open the door. "No, Britney!" I yelled at her, reaching for the door. "Oh Mila, we can't very well be rude." She turned the knob, and as soon as it was slightly open, we saw a tall, thin, handsome Hispanic man in the door.

"Hi Breetteney, hi Meela," he smiled at both of us. "I yam Carlos."

"Just how in the world could you know our names?" Britney flirted with Carlos as I bolted for the door. Another man, who we would come to know as Rodrigo, grabbed me and pinned me down on my bed.

"Chico tol me dat you cou be feisty, Mila. Why you try to run away from such a nice guy?" Carlos whispered into my ear as he pushed my face into the unmade bed, and moved my hair away from my face with his slimy hands. "You should know you can't run from Chico. I yam his cuzeen, and I yam here to collect."

Rodrigo held back Britney while Carlos stripped off my pants and underwear and raped me from behind. I fought back the best I could, but I was basically powerless.

Britney cried out when she saw what was happening to me, and Rodrigo made her watch. "You'll be next, Britney," he laughed at her.

They hurried us out of the motel room, down the stairs, and into their car. They put the child locks on the door so we couldn't open them, and forced us to get down in the car so no one would see us. I didn't know where we were going because I couldn't see the road signs. Britney just kept sobbing. She couldn't even look at me. I didn't have a watch on, and hours or minutes could have passed before we pulled into a garage.

"Get up, *putas*." The men pushed us out of the car and into their house. It was a medium sized townhouse, two bedrooms, two bathrooms, a kitchen and a living room. It seemed like the kind of place a nice, young family might live.

"Chico tellz me you are prosteetutes, jes? Well, you still owe Chico a lot of money, Mila. You and your friend here can work off your debt togeder. You weel start tonight. And don't eben theenk ov trying to get away, seelly Mila. Ju know I weel find you whereber you go."

With that, Carlos and silent Rodrigo closed all the blinds, left the house, and padlocked us inside.

Britney began to cry again. I tried to console her, to apologize for the mess we were in.

"Oh Mila, how could you apologize? It's not your fault. I wish Carlos had taken me instead of you." Her whole body shook as she cried.

"No, Britney, it is my fault. I owe Chico money, and he is taking revenge on you for helping me leave him."

"Oh Mila, I don't care about the money. I owe lots of people money, too. Chico sure is a bad apple though, darlin', and I don't like the company he keeps." Even after all that Britney had seen and done at the VIP, she still had a blindly optimistic view of the world. I loved her for that, even if it was her naiveté that opened the motel door to Carlos.

We brainstormed ways to get out of the house, but couldn't find one that worked. We had no choice but to spend the day there, awaiting our fate that night.

The daylight eventually turned to night, and Carlos and Rodrigo came back for us. Carlos took me in his car, and Rodrigo took Britney. They had brought clothes for us to change into. They didn't cover much more than my "dancing clothes" did at the VIP. Except this time, there wasn't going to be a stage.

As we drove toward our destination, Carlos threatened me. He told me that I could not leave until I paid off the debt that I owed to Chico, and that if I tried to run away again, he would cut out my tongue and send it to my mother, Adela, in Bratislava. He had somehow found out her name and address, and told me that in addition to sending her my tongue, he would rape her himself. I couldn't let that happen to my mother. All she had ever tried to do was make a good life for me. I would do what I was asked, I would repay my debt, and then I would get the hell out.

It is very hard to talk about what came next. I was brought to a trailer that night, and I was forced to have sex with 18 different men. Some of them were gentle, but mostly they were clumsy, drunk, or brutish. They hurt me, and some of them refused to wear condoms. It was already light out when Carlos opened the door and told me that I could return home with him. I didn't know which was worse, staying in the trailer or returning to his townhouse with him. I was too tired to care much at that point.

Britney arrived back at the house a little while after us. We were sharing a twin bed in the smaller bedroom, and I made room in the bed for her. She took off her "work clothes" and got into bed in her underwear. We hugged and cried, too shocked and sad to speak. We cuddled into each other for support, and eventually fell asleep.

The next day was more of the same, and the day after that, too. I learned that Britney had a little girl back in Kentucky named Savannah, who lived with Britney's mom. She would be 8 years old now.

Rodrigo told Britney that he would rape her himself if she tried to leave. Carlos took our cell phones, and the apartment didn't have a phone. Even if it did, so what? Who would we call? Britney knew that as a prostitute, she would go to jail if she got caught, and me, well, I had let my visa expire, so the police would send me straight back to Bratislava, and everyone would know that I had sex for money. My mother would be so ashamed. We didn't have access to a phone, and there was no way out. We were stuck.

Chapter 24

Lily

It is truly amazing where life takes us. I got a group of law enforcement, social service providers, and members of local women's organizations together to begin addressing the problem of where to place women who flee domestic violence or other immigrants who escape from torture, persecution, exploitation and abuse when there is no affordable housing to be found. We figured we might have better luck if we approached the problem as a team. We've decided to meet twice a month somewhere in the Panhandle, a different city each time.[48] We call ourselves "The Taskforce." Very official, right? I brought up the idea of shortening it to "The Force" and getting matching uniforms, or badges, or T-shirts, or even capes, but no one was into it. You'd be amazed how humorless you can become when you work with people whose lives have been torn apart by others. I understand how easy it is to feel down about all the pain and violence in our clients' lives. Their experiences are undeniably heartbreaking. I guess what drives me to keep going is a bit of irreverence, being able to laugh, without losing sight of the urgency of the issues at hand.

The Taskforce wants to eventually take on all kinds of issues of exploitation, but right now we are trying to focus our efforts on the need for shelter for my clients (who are also the patients, victims and witnesses of members of The Force). I want a shelter that is safe and therapeutic, a place my clients could call home for a while, that would

---

48. This can get complicated. Did you know that Florida actually fits into two different time zones? The time switches somewhere in the Panhandle. I discovered this phenomenon once when I had clients that always arrived an hour late. Being half Latin American myself, I brushed it off as cultural difference; the clients explained that it was a state mandate. Then we hugged. Or maybe it didn't happen like that at all, but still, it's important for you to know, in case you find yourself in the Panhandle, and you have an important appointment: make sure you both know what time it is for real. If this book teaches you nothing else, you will always have this nugget of wisdom.

also keep out the bad guys. Some of the police officers want to keep the clients in a place where they could be accessible as witnesses to the prosecution, if a big bust or something ended up going down. We each have our different goals, but ultimately, all of us want the same thing for our clients.

After a few months of giving speeches, it felt like I had spoken to every last person in town or within a few hundred mile radius with money to contribute to the shelter. People gave as generously as they could, but it will take a long time to raise enough to build the kind of place that could provide everything my clients are likely to need. In the meantime, one of the officers came up with the idea of dedicating one cell of the local jail to domestic violence victims. It's a big step down from what I wanted,[49] but it's something. It has a separate entrance, a shower, a few sets of bunk beds, a little kitchen, and lots of security. It's not anywhere close to enough, but it's a start.

Last week, I had just come back from the most recent Taskforce meeting and was settling into some legal work when I had the pleasure to meet the most engaging and delightful sheriff. Jim Kerrigan. His skin was leathery looking, toughened by the sun, and he was dressed like he was poised for a covert operation in the desert. Jim had been in 'Nam and his speech was a mix of southern twang and Army speak. He had heard about The Taskforce from some other police folk, and he wanted in.

"Mrs. Stone," he began, entering unannounced and without an appointment, "I hear you have been doin' some mighty fine work around these parts."

Despite his bold entrance, or maybe because of it, I liked Jim immediately. He knew how flattery would work with me. He continued in this forthright, but gentlemanly manner.

"My name is Jim, Jim Kerrigan. I'm the sheriff in Polkaloosa County just a few hours due west of here. You ever been to my county, Mrs. Stone?"

---

49. I mean, let's face it folks. Would you want to spend the night in jail after leaving an abusive spouse? It's hard to describe just how far from ideal this situation is, but it was the best we could do at the time, and it was a start. It was a safe place with a soft bed, food and a shower.

I told him that in fact, I had never been, but I heard it was lovely this time of year. Bless his heart, Sheriff Jim Kerrigan, he didn't pick up on my Yankee-inflected sarcasm.

"It sure is beautiful, Mrs. Stone."

"Please," I interrupted, "call me Lily." I had actually never heard anyone call me Mrs. Stone before. I had heard "Attorney Lily" and "*Abogada* Lily" for my Spanish speaking clients, and "Lily Walker Stone," when being introduced at one of the groups I was speaking to about building a shelter, but never Mrs. Stone. Mrs. Stone was my mother-in-law, I thought. I guess it is me too, now.

"Okay then, Miss Lily, you can call me Jim as well. Polkaloosa, Miss Lily, isn't much to speak of this time of year, but I tell you what, in the spring, the dogwoods and azaleas are in full bloom, and it sure does look like heaven."

Well, as much as I liked hearing about the foliage of Polkaloosa County in the springtime, I had a very nice client waiting for me. He was applying for derivative asylum based on his wife's approved asylum from Haiti. Alfonse hadn't yet received his work authorization, and so he was the primary caretaker of his two little girls, aged 3 and 4. They had poor Alfonse pretending to be a choo choo train and they were jumping up and down on their eager-to-please conductor/dad when Jim and I started to chat. I tried to move our conversation along.

Jim took one look at poor Alfonse, heard his screaming little girls, and beat me to the punch.

"Miss Lily, much as I'd like to stay here all day and talk, I can see that you are busy, so I'll make this brief. I have heard rumblings about some illegals working in post-Katrina reconstruction along the Panhandle."

I bristled at the word "illegals." I know a lot of people use that word and don't mean anything by it, but people also use the word to dehumanize immigrants, and make them seem like they aren't people, just "illegals" that don't have any right to be here, so we can do to them and dispose of them as we see fit. Really, though, folks, there is no such thing as an "illegal" human being. Yes, there are people in this country who lack the proper papers and who don't have the correct immigration status, but I would never call them "aliens" or "illegals." Maybe Jim misunderstood our organization's name? The Immigrant Justice Center of Hiawassee Springs was for justice for immigrants, not justice from "illegals." Suddenly, as much as I found Jim charming, I wasn't so sure that we were on the same side of the situation. I listened for more cues.

"Apparently, lots of enterprisin' young Americans are bringing in carloads of Mexicans and other Central Americans to fix up houses in Mississippi and Louisiana, and now parts of Florida, too, including some areas along the water in Polkaloosa County. And, the way these Americans make all their money is that they don't actually pay the workers anything."

Now I was getting a bit angry. First, Jim is worrying about "illegals" around here, and now he was basically saying that these "illegals" are so stupid that they would just work for nothing? Come on now, Jim.

"Um, sheriff, with all due respect, do you mean to tell me that American citizens are going into neighborhoods in Mexico and Guatemala and Nicaragua and Honduras, convincing people to leave their families to come and work in the U.S., and then they don't pay them? And you think these workers wouldn't just get up and leave?" Jim's theory seemed preposterous to me, but I tried my best to be respectful.

"I know it sounds farfetched, Miss Lily, but it's a bit more complicated than that. You see, these American contractors and companies tell the workers that they will pay them, as soon as they pay off their passage to the U.S. But, then they get to the Gulf Coast, and the Americans charge them for rent, and for their ride to and from the construction sites, and for food, and the next thing you know, the Americans tell them that they owe even more. And the thing is, these illegals aren't like the politicians in office, who have no problem rackin' up a big debt over in Iraq, saddling our grandbabies with all that."

Finally, I could see eye to eye with Jim.

"No, Miss Lily, these illegals are good, honest folks who believe that when a debt is owed, they need to pay it back right then. So, they live like sardines all packed into a house, with hundreds of other workers, and these good, honest men work all day without pay. I tell you what else. There are some other men looking to make a pretty penny, and they recognize that these boys coming up from Mexico and those countries are going to get pretty lonely without their women around. So, they got this idea to set up brothels around the camps. They have trailers, and the men come to visit these women for thirty bucks each, they get to spend fifteen minutes forgetting about their troubles for a while in the arms of a nice, young woman, who also isn't actually getting paid to be there. We need to stop this."

Jim was back in my good graces, and I wanted in.

"Absolutely, Jim. This is awful. What can I do to help?"

"Miss Lily, I want into The Taskforce, and I want you on my legal team while we stomp this one out. We need a Spanish speaker to help translate. My men and I are calling this Operation HoneyBear."

Finally, someone with a sense of humor on The Taskforce. I bet I could convince Jim that we needed matching capes.

"Sounds great, Jim," I said, and we shook on it.

"I'll be in touch, Miss, Lily, and I'll see you at the next Taskforce meeting in two weeks, you hear?" He put his cowboy hat back on, tipped it in my direction, patted Alfonse's little girls on their heads, and was out the door.

New Beginnings

Chapter 25

Rosa

Hiawassee Springs, Florida
March 4, 2007

Querida Diary,

Time passed and I continued on. I was not really living, but I was alive, if that makes sense. I continued despite the pain and the hurt so that I could eventually get out of here. I missed Mami. I missed Ana. Just as I had almost given up, things took a different turn.

You see, Marco had been all this time without a job. I know that he must have felt angry about it, because he took it out on me. Just last week he told me that he got word of a good job working in the ship-building industry in a place called Panacea. Marco is good with his hands, and he helped an uncle work on ships when he was a boy. He decided to take the job, and it was understood that I would follow him. What other choice did I have?

If Marco hadn't taken this job, I don't know what would have happened. There were times when I didn't believe I could go on another day. Those times are over.

It turns out that there were many people being taken advantage of who were working on building ships, and doing other construction work in the area. I had no idea. There had been a really bad storm, a hurricane, and lots of people lost their homes, and then the people needed new homes and businesses built, so people came from all over to build things. Some of those people who came to work did not have legal documents and people took advantage of them. Some of them weren't being paid anything at all. There were workers' barracks by

146

the ships where Marco was supposed to stay, but instead, we mainly stayed in his car, and then he would crack open the window and lock me in the car all day. I hid on the floor so no one would see me. It was hot and miserable.

I tried to sleep most of the day, since I had to work all night. I was always exhausted, but it was hard to sleep, because the floor of the car was uneven and the heat and humidity were overwhelming. Occasionally, out of boredom, I would lift my head and carefully peek out the window, so as to see but not to be seen. I would catch glimpses of the ships, or the men hammering things on the site. A few times I saw an older white man walking around. He also seemed as if he preferred to watch rather than have people notice him. I wondered what he was doing there, and whether he was the big boss of the whole operation. He had an important walk.

It turned out that that particular white man was not the boss of the construction project at all. Instead, he was trying to stop what was happening, since he found out that Marco and some of the others were not being paid what they deserved, and the bosses were thieves who were stealing the money and the labor from the workers. This white man's name was Jim, he is a policeman, and meeting him changed my life. We didn't actually meet at first, it was more like he found me. I probably stared at him from the car parked next to the construction site longer than I should have, and maybe he felt my eyes on him. One day, after months of sneaking views of him, Jim finally saw me.

He saw me, sitting in the car, locked in, and he tried to talk to me. I didn't know enough English to communicate with him then, so I was scared, and I hid from him when he tried to open the door. He couldn't open it because Marco locked me in and kept the key on him during the day. Either way, I was too scared to answer him, and maybe he could tell that I didn't understand, because he left. I was so relieved. Then, a little while later, maybe an hour or so, he came back with a woman. She looked like a white woman, too, but surprisingly she spoke to me in Spanish through the small opening in the rear passenger door window. Her name is Lily, and she is a lawyer. Abogada Lily looked like a yanqui, and she told me that she was American, but she spoke Spanish like a Porteña, like she came from Buenos Aires, my capital city. I didn't want to talk to her until Jim the police officer went away. Even then I don't know why I trusted her, but I did. She had a nice face, and maybe I was too tired to keep up with my life anymore; it was too hot in that car. Still, I knew that Abogada Lily only came because that police officer had called her. Were they working together to trick me? Marco had warned me, just like the Cuencas did, that if the police found me, they would put me in jail forever. My life felt like jail, though, even though I do not believe that Marco really wished me any harm. Still, I had given up: I didn't care what happened to me anymore.

Abogada Lily and Jim got me out of that car, they took me to an office a few towns away, and we talked for a long time. Once I started talking, I didn't know how to stop. I told Abogada Lily and Jim all about Mami and Ana and the Cuencas and finally about Marco. It was hours later when I was finally done talking, or so it seemed. Abogada Lily and Jim told me that they would take me to a safe place, but when their car stopped in front of the local jail, I knew it was a trap. I unlocked the car door and started to run. I couldn't believe it, that the Cuencas and Marco were right!

Jim caught up with me first and caught me in a kind of hug where he kept repeating the only Spanish phrase I think he knew to calm me down, "Todo bien, todo bien, todo bien," except it sounded more like "Toad-a-bean," and I continued feeling scared, caught like

a "toad," and I struggled away from him. Abogada Lily caught up a
bit later, calmed me down and explained the situation. I can't say
that I completely trusted them, as I walked in the jail's back entrance
toward my living quarters. Abogada Lily kept trying to convince me
that it was a "shelter" and that it was only temporary, but it did not
seem like a nice place to stay. There were bars on the outside of my
room, just like a prison. There were good things about the jail, though.
I didn't see any other people, like other criminals there, and there was
a clean, warm, soft bed with pillows that I wanted to sleep on forever.
After a few days, I started to feel some relief that Marco wasn't around
anymore, and that I could just sleep through the nights without having to be with men.

In that cell, though, I started to really miss Mami, Ana and
Maria. Me senti sola, I felt alone. And even though Abogada Lily
would come by and check on me once a day, and Jim would also stop
by and do his very best to communicate with me, for the first time in
a while, Diary, I really was on my own.

Rosa

Chapter 26

Mila

Britney and I worked for months without end. Carlos always took me around, and Rodrigo took her. Every night we would work, from late in the evening until the sun would begin to rise the next day. After a long night of work, we would sleep for most of the next day, shielding our faces from the light pouring through the blinds. Once in a while I would try to pretend that I was Julia Roberts, with that wealthy client in *Pretty Woman*, but reality was so far from that fairy tale, that I couldn't keep up the act for long. Nights became our days. Where my acting ability used to save me, I now turned to something stronger. I grew to hate the sunset, knowing it would be the start of another terrible night. I drank more and more with the "clients," a sip or chug or puff of whatever they would give me. It numbed the pain a bit, at least for a little while.

After a few weeks, I started to feel foolish for trying to leave Chico. He wasn't perfect, but he was strong and handsome and at least I could go home at the end of a hard day of work at my two jobs and find a welcome partner in bed. Being with Chico was the last time that I had sex because I wanted to, and not because I was forced. I didn't see a way out of this situation, a way back into the world of consensual sex and hopes of life as an actress in New York. I felt worthless. So many times I thought about ending it all. If a client went to the bathroom I would search the pockets of his discarded pants for pills, never finding a sufficient number quickly enough to do the trick. I don't know whether I would have actually done it, if I would have found enough pills at any given time. Maybe I didn't really have the guts. Carlos knew where my mother lived, and I was scared that he would hurt her if I didn't pay off my debt to him. I had to keep working. I had to see my way out of this mess to either return to my mother, or follow my dreams to New York City.

I wonder now how much longer I would have gone on like that if I hadn't met Jim. He came as a client, dressed and acted like one. I was only allowed to spend fifteen minutes with each client before Carlos would knock on the door, and the client would have to leave to make room for the next customer. Jim came into the room, and locked the door.

"Good evening, ma'am," he said, tipping his large cowboy hat to me.

I replied with the script I had been taught. "Good evening, handsome. What would you like tonight?"

This man seemed different, but I had seen all kinds. The men I served were mainly immigrants themselves, mostly from Mexico and other countries down there, doing construction or working in the fields. Still, I had also seen men of all races, ages, and social class coming for their time with me in the trailer. Sometimes Carlos would rent a motel room for the night instead. It was all the same to me.

"I'd like to talk to you, if that's okay." The tall Caucasian man made no effort to touch me, or remove his pants. I was confused.

"Anything you like I can do." I was trying my best, but I said my lines with half a heart, and anyway, he didn't seem interested in sex. I sat down on the bed and patted the space next to my exposed thigh. He didn't budge from his folding chair on the other side of the small space.

"What is your name?" he asked, in a serious voice, one not interested in playing games.

I knew that Carlos gave the clients the drill about the fifteen minute rule, but this one seemed keen to waste his time on questions. It was about two in the morning, I had been working since 6 p.m., and I was okay to let him spend his allotted time however he liked.

"What would you like my name to be?" I smiled at him, or at least I tried to. It had been a good long while since I had felt my face flex into a natural smile, or at least, smiled without thinking about how to force my muscles into a proper smile shape. I tried to be convincing. He continued to seem unamused, and indifferent. He kept glancing at his watch, a black and orange rubber number, not the flashy gold and silver I had seen on other customers who acted fancy, like they were paying for sex with me as a start to a more permanent relationship where they could afford to buy me nice things.

"Would you like to get out of here? You seem like a nice girl. Why don't you come with me?"

I tried to pretend like I wouldn't have rather been anywhere but there. He wasn't the first man to come see me for sex and then try to get me to leave with him. In the ten months I had been working in Florida, I had heard most every line, and I had been offered the world.

"Come home to Mexico with me, you will meet my family and be my wife." Right. I had heard it all before. I had no way of telling them that I couldn't leave without getting in worse trouble with Carlos. And, there was no way of knowing whether life would actually be better with them instead.

Carlos told me that he would always come and find me. He told me every day that I still owed him and Chico money. He made it clear to me after not too long that Chico had never applied for an extension to my visa, that I was no longer in America legally, and that the police would get me even if he didn't find me first. I had seen in Bratislava what the police were capable of. How could I have been so foolish? New York felt farther away to me now than it had when I was back in Bratislava.

I had wandered so far into my thoughts that I forgot that the man in the big hat was still in the room. The clock was ticking. He sat next to me on the bed and gently, but firmly, placed a thumb under my chin so that I was looking him in the eye.

"Listen to me closely. I think you aren't here because you want to be here. I think someone is making you be here. I am with the police, and I am not going to hurt you." At that moment, I wanted to scream or run away, but I felt like, "Okay, Mila, the game is up. You were in America illegally, and the police found you. Turn yourself in."

I was too tired to fight anymore. I just wanted to go to sleep for a very long time, and at that moment, I wasn't sure that I ever wanted to wake up.

"I am Jim. Sherriff Jim Kerrigan. Tell me your name. Your real name." He said it gently, almost like he was asking me for a favor instead of commanding me to give him something potentially dangerous to me.

"I am Mila. Mila Gulej." I spoke tentatively, almost as if I wasn't sure of who I was anymore. It felt like I was asking a question, instead of asserting myself.

"Well, Mila, would you like to get out of here?" Was he serious? Of course I wanted out of that hellhole, but where to from there? How would I ever pay back my debts? Wouldn't they come find me eventually?

I nodded with a half smile, unable to fully explain all the questions still in my head. What would happen to me? To Britney? To our families if Chico and his buddies ever found us again? I nodded without thinking.

In a matter of minutes, Jim spoke into his jacket, called his "backup" and the trailer was surrounded. What happened next flashed by in a blur. Jim showed me that he had a gun, grabbed me under the arm, and said, "Play along." I felt like I was acting in my own thriller.

We exited the room, and I saw Carlos being handcuffed to my left, wrestling with two police officers, and one of them was a woman! Jim rushed me out of the trailer and into a car that was waiting there. He gently pushed my head downward into the car, protecting me from bumping into the frame of the back left passenger door. He closed the car door, and for a brief second, I was alone in the backseat.

I felt giddy to be free of Carlos, but confused about what else I wanted out of life. Could I trust Jim? Where was he taking me? Could I help Britney now? Would I go back to Bratislava? Would I ever tell my mother about all of this? Would anyone ever believe me?

Chapter 27

Lily

Rosa and Mila are what we would legally refer to as victims of human trafficking. Through my work with Jim on Operation HoneyBear, I learned a great deal about the different kinds and levels of exploitation involved in trafficking, and I became more sensitized to it in my practice. I also started to understand more about why men who were not getting paid would stay at a job to pay off debt, and why a woman would stay with a man who hit her and made her prostitute herself. I learned about Stockholm Syndrome, where victims of hostage situations or kidnappings come to positively associate themselves with their captors, and sometimes even love the very people that keep them captive. I finally understood why Rosa and Mila wouldn't have made more attempts to flee, despite the terrible situations they found themselves in. Mila certainly did not love Carlos, nor did Rosa love Marco, not in any real sense of the word. Still, Rosa was a virgin before she met Marco, and she felt like he was her boyfriend, even if he was not a very good one.

I owe a great deal to Officer Jim and his team for connecting the dots in the Panhandle. They knew that large numbers of men working hard away from their families might inspire underground businesses to service them. Jim and his team scoured the Gulf Coast searching for any evidence that women were being commercially sexually exploited. They unearthed an anthill, with all kinds of human scum like Carlos and Marco and countless others trying to make a buck off of someone vulnerable. They found a gang of Moldovans that had brought in five girls, all under the age of fourteen, and they had not been let out of their brothel for nine months. The girls were pale, undernourished, and badly in need of medical attention. Those poor girls. In time I became the attorney for each of them as well.

I also credit Jim Kerrigan for having the wherewithal and the collaborative spirit necessary to involve an immigration lawyer in this whole business. For the purpose of adequate victim care, sometimes it really is important for female clients to have a woman to talk to, especially since Jim is not the cuddliest of ex-military men, despite his best efforts.

After Jim found Rosa in the car, and I stayed to coax her out,[50] I called Jim to tell him that a young man named "Marco" had been the one who locked Rosa in that car. Jim went on the hunt around the construction site and when he found Marco, he charged him with violations of the Mann Act[51] and false imprisonment, just for starters. After Jim brought Marco to the Panacea local police station, he called me.

"Miss Lily, I brought in that stupid kid who was keeping Rosa hostage. I tell you what, Miss Lily, I wanted to rip that sorry little bastard a new one. Pardon my French, Miss Lily."

"No problem, Jim. I didn't even know you spoke French."

"I don't speak French, Miss Lily, I meant to apologize for my coarse language while speaking with a lady. Anyway, Lily, Marco has stepped in it big time. I am going to charge him with the intentional prostituting of a minor as well as being an accomplice to the Cuenca family's trafficking of a minor. I'll need you to comb over the finer points of human trafficking law and make sure we are on the same page before the feds get in here and muck it up."

"Fair enough, Jim, but isn't this a lot of federal law anyway? Is this really our jurisdiction?"

"Miss Lily, yes it is federal law, but where are the feds right now? Sometimes we have to take care of our own backyards. And as for Marco, well, the feds are likely to give him a deal for fingerin' the Cuencas. I tell you, Miss Lily, I'd like to hog tie that boy to my car and drive him around town for what he did to poor Rosa. That kid was stupid enough to work for a shipbuilding company that wasn't paying him squat, but he sure found a way to supplement his income with Rosa's 'customers.'"

---

50. Which coincidentally is not something they taught us how to do in law school

51. Have you heard of the Mann Act before? It's a relic from our American legal past and basically banned the interstate transport of women and girls for "immoral purposes." Before Congress created good anti-human trafficking legislation, we used to rely on this bad boy.

I went to visit Rosa and Mila in the shelter, which, unfortunately, is still that space in the rear of the local jail. Rome wasn't built in a day, and neither is a shelter in a poor, rural part of America. Donations have arrived, and we are getting there, but it isn't happening as fast as anyone would like. I have travelled around the state checking out different domestic violence and homeless shelters to figure out what we need to build in Hiawassee Springs. We need so much more than we have money for right now. You know how little girls have their Barbie Dream House? I have my Lily Dream Shelter, with multilingual staff, therapists and doctors and support groups on hand. I went to one domestic violence shelter in the south part of the state that called their clients "guests" and let them choose from different "services" offered as if it were a spa. They had separate apartments for each "guest" with various amenities. One day. One day we will bring that kind of care to the good people of the 'wassee. God knows they deserve it. Until then, other kinds of progress are moving life forward.

After a few weeks in the jail cell, Rosa decided that she wanted to help Jim prosecute the Cuencas and Marco for what they did to her. Thank goodness, the U.S. Congress created a pathway toward citizenship for folks in Mila and Rosa's situation. It is called the Trafficking Victims Protection Act, or TVPA for short. Basically, if someone is forced to work against their will[52] and they are willing to help law enforcement with the prosecution of their traffickers, then they can stay in the U.S. Children like Rosa who were commercially sexually exploited actually are not required to aid in the prosecution of the people who hurt them, but Rosa has decided to help anyway.

Does all that legal mumbo jumbo sound complicated? In practice, it is more than complicated. There is an intricate web of players involved. There are the local police (like Jim), the federal police (the Federal Bureau of Investigation and Immigration and Customs Enforcement folks), and the attorneys (which can be state attorneys, fed-

---

52. Either in the agricultural industry, or as a domestic servant, or in commercial sex, etc.

eral attorneys from the Department of Justice and the U.S. Attorney's office as well as immigration attorneys like me). But wait, there's more. After you finish with all of the attorneys and the law enforcement folks, then there are the benefits people from Health and Human Services (HHS). Once they say that someone is a certified victim of human trafficking, they are entitled to a few hundred dollars a month for four months.[53] HHS then has contracts with local nonprofits who dole out the cash to victims of trafficking, and sometimes help them make budgets, set up bank accounts, learn the public transportation routes, and how to spend their money wisely. In a budget crunch, those service organizations lack the time and the person power necessary to shepherd a recent victim through the process of getting used to life in the USA. I can't help but shake my head at the news reports I hear now of victims being "freed" and "rescued." Yes, it is a great thing to help a trafficked person exit the conditions of their exploitation. But it is only the beginning of the process. Life after trafficking is not a seamless transition.

Rosa and I spent a good bit of time together, and I think we built up enough trust for her to believe that I was her advocate, and that I wanted her to make whatever decisions she thought were best for her, given all the information. After about three weeks of getting to know each other, the first nitty gritty conversation Rosa and I had about her legal options went a little something like this (translated into English):

> me: So, Rosa, have you thought about whether you would like to stay here or return to Argentina? Either way is fine, and we can make it work for you.

> Rosa: I have. I need to get out of this jail and get back to work so I can repay my debt to Marco. I guess it would be easier for me to do that here, because it is hard to make a lot of money back home. It would take even longer to pay back Marco then.

---

53. Yeah, because after coming from a different country, not speaking the language, being exposed to God knows what during months or years of exploitation, abuse and neglect, it just takes four months to get over trauma and get a job and move on. Uh, not exactly.

me: Oh Rosa. First, you are not in jail. I promise. I know it looks like jail, and well, it is technically a jail, but this is a shelter, a safe place where you will be free from harm and can start moving on with your life.

Rosa: Right, a shelter, not a jail. Okay. But can I leave soon to repay my debt? I owe Marco a lot of money and my family might be in danger if I don't pay it off.

me: (*Gently, with as much patience as I could muster*) Rosa, you do not have to pay back anything. You no longer owe any money to anyone. In fact, you never owed any money – they just said that to manipulate you. Do you understand me? Rosa, you don't have to stay here if you don't want to. It's just that housing can be expensive, and this way it is free, and you can focus on other things besides work.

Rosa: Attorney Lily, you are very kind and I am grateful for your help, but you do not understand. My mother and sister will be in danger if I do not pay off this debt. Please, I need to find a way to make money.

me: Rosa, you haven't been able to make your own choices for a while, but now you can choose again. You can either stay in the U.S. or you can return to Argentina. If you want to stay, we can bring your mother and sister here to be with you.[54] Would you like that?

Rosa: All I want in the world is to go home, to be with my mother and sister. I am scared, though, that the Cuencas have friends and family in Jujuy, and that they will always come back for me, and for the money I owe them. I think *Mami* and Maria would be safer here, with me. But we would need to live somewhere else besides jail.

It took many more conversations like that. For Rosa, the idea of working off a debt was so ingrained into her cultural reality that it

---

54. For the record, since Rosa was eligible for a T visa, and she is a minor, she is also eligible to bring her parents or minor siblings as "T visa derivatives" to the U.S.

took a long time for her to understand that she had long paid off any debt that she once owed. To anyone. She ultimately decided to stay here, and we began the process of applying for "derivative" visas for her sister and mother, who still didn't quite understand how it was that they could come to the U.S. as well. They still secretly believed that it was the generous Cuencas who were making it all possible for their family, and mentioned the beneficent Cuencas in their prayers each week, thanking God for their good fortune.

Marco and the Cuencas were picked up by the FBI. The Cuencas were being held in a lovely local establishment with bars on the windows in Miami, and Marco was staying in a similar "hotel" located about an eight hour drive to the north of the state. While we waited for her criminal case against the Cuencas and Marco to move forward, and with her abusers safely behind bars, Rosa began to breathe a bit easier and restarted her efforts to learn English. I helped her enroll in the local English as a Second Language (ESL) program. She, tentatively at first, made friends. She studied English with every second that she had, catching up for lost time spent not learning, not being the creative and intelligent child that she had always been. In some respects, Rosa thrived; at other times, there were setbacks.

My husband picked up some extra cash during the slow summers by teaching two nights a week in the ESL program. Rosa was his favorite student. I never discuss my clients with anyone, not even Josh, so he had no way of knowing that Rosa was his student and my client as well. He shared some of her writing with me. She wrote poetry and prose, mainly about Ana, who she said, "never was far from her heart or her smile." She wrote beautifully.

Within months, and still waiting to see what would happen in the criminal case against the Cuencas, Rosa began 9th grade at Hiawassee Springs High. High school is a huge challenge for Rosa, having spent much time out of the classroom and speaking English as her second language. She is several years older than the other freshman, and normally, she wouldn't be allowed to start 9th grade at the age of sixteen. Without revealing my client's confidences, I explained to the school why they should make an exception for Rosa, and they have done so on a probationary basis, dependent on her academic performance. I do not worry about Rosa making the grade. She takes nothing for granted, and studies night and day to catch up to her classmates, her excitement for competition and learning renewed.

Rosa continues to write in her journal, to keep a record of all she has seen and done in America. In May, she wrote about her first high school dance. I was honored to go with her to buy her first dress, but sad that her mother and sister couldn't see her looking so beautiful, as they were still waiting for the local consulate to issue their travel documents. Rosa picked out an emerald green dress, and she looked beautiful. I wished her mom could have seen her shine. Here is an excerpt from her journal that she agreed to share about her excitement for that night:

May 29, 2007

Dear Diary,

America has become much more of the place that I wanted it to be. Where is Ana now? Can she see me, sitting in class with my hand raised to answer questions? In English! Mami and Maria are on their way to me, and we are going to live together in Florida. Diary, it has been a long road, you know, but things seem to have more sun now.

I am going to a dance! My first dance! In school, this dance is very important to the students. They have groups of people who work on the music, and other students work to make the room look nice and festive. There is a nice boy named Philip who asked me to go to the dance with him. His parents are from China and he talks less than the others. He is an immigrant, too. His parents came to teach math at the local university. His face turned very pink when he asked me, so of course I said yes to him. The other girls in the class think Philip likes me, but I don't know. I hope so!

I will write more soon,

Rosa

Chapter 28

Mila

Officer Jim saved me that night. Maybe I could have gone on forever, but I felt like something inside me had broken. It has been a few months since then, and that brokenness still sits inside me. Sometimes all I can do is sit and cry. Sometimes I can't get out of bed for days, feeling the pain of the scars inside. But sometimes, and there are days, I still feel sad, but I can also feel the beginning of something better. On those days I start to hope again, I start to make plans and look toward the future with something like excitement.

In case you were wondering, the last I heard from Britney, she had agreed to testify against Rodrigo and Carlos and she and her daughter are in the witness protection program. That's all I know. I hope they are in Montana. I saw it on a map and it looks far enough away from here that Chico and his army of jerks will never find them.

Since Jim took me away from Carlos, I share a room with another girl. She is a few years younger than me, and her name is Rosa. At first, we could barely talk to each other, because she did not really speak English, and I only know a little Spanish from Chico. All I knew was that Rosa seemed sad, she wrote in her journal a lot, she had nightmares that made her scream out loud, and we were sharing the "shelter" room in a jail cell. Attorney Lily got us a television set, and we would watch the *telenovelas* together. Whenever we weren't watching the television, Rosa was usually writing in that journal, or studying English. She was shy to talk to me, but after a while, she decided to try. Maybe it was to practice her English, maybe it was to reach out to another person.

"Mila," she began, one day while we watched our favorite *telenovela*, "why does Maria Elena keep going back to Manuel when he is not nice to her?" She asked me with a shy smile, an obvious effort to be friendly, and a rhetorical question at best. We both knew why sometimes it was hard to end an unhealthy relationship. Rosa was the first to break the otherwise calm, respectful quiet of our non-verbal communication. These were her first words to me.

Over the next few months, we didn't talk a lot. It was hard to share a small, closed in space with someone I could barely communicate with. Every once in a while, though, Rosa would share bits and pieces of her life. I learned how much she liked empanadas, and once Attorney Lily found out, she brought freshly made ones to us. She knew that I wanted to be an actress, and she often told me that I was pretty enough to do it. We wondered about what we would do after we left "the shelter." I used to joke with her that she would write the stories, and I would act them out in the movies. It felt good to connect to someone who didn't know about all the terrible things that I had done. Tentatively at first, we started to laugh again.

Attorney Lily wants me to help Officer Jim and the police put Chico, Carlos and Rodrigo behind bars. I don't really want to. I mean, I really want them to pay for all that they did to me and to Britney, but I don't want to see them again. I just want to forget them, forget those terrible years of my life, and move on to the big city. I really want to speak to my mother again, but I still haven't called her. I don't want her to know what has happened with me. And even if I tried to tell her, I don't even know where I'd begin.

Officer Jim tried to convince me that it was the right thing to do, to help him and the other attorneys make Chico pay for what he had done to me and to stop him doing it to others. For as much as I hated him, I didn't care to see him punished if it meant that I had to see him again, to testify against him in court. I only wanted to move on, but trying to put Chico behind bars would mean that I would have to tell my story to every new attorney, every new policeman on the case. I didn't want to do it.

I was right, by the way, that Chico never renewed my visa in the U.S., and that I had long overstayed my legal permit. During my first few days at the "shelter," I figured they would deport me at any time. Attorney Lily let me know about the different ways I could try to stay legally if I wanted to. Of course I wanted to. How could I go home and face my mother after all that I had done? How could I face anyone back in Bratislava? How could I go back to working in that same restaurant, serving dumplings, like nothing at all had happened? Plain and simple: I couldn't, and I wouldn't.

My feelings about the Chico situation didn't change throughout my talks with Attorney Lily. Still, one thought plagued me: I didn't want what happened to me to ever happen to anyone ever again. Attorney Lily assured me that the only way to stop people like Chico and Carlos and Rodrigo from doing all the horrible things that they did to me is to prosecute them – to bring their actions to light – and then to make them pay for their deeds by taking them out of society and putting them into prison. Lily explained that my family would receive protection and not suffer as a result of my telling my story.

Still, I was torn. I had so much anger inside me from the things that Carlos made me do. I was never an angry person, and I hated the rage that swirled inside. Maybe, if telling them to their faces how much I hated them could help me put that anger aside, and protect other people, then maybe I would go to court. I needed more time to think about it.

We started my application for a T visa, which is a visa for a victim of human trafficking. That was me. It turns out I was a victim. Attorney Lily prefers to use the term "survivor," but let's face it, I had had some bad things happen to me and I was still around to talk about it. I guess we were both right.

Once we started the process for me to be able to stay in the U.S. legally, I talked with Attorney Lily a lot about my dreams of becoming an actress and moving to New York City. She was excited for me, but told me that I should stay around until the criminal case against Chico and his group got going, and suggested that I study theatre at the local university while I had free housing at the shelter. It seemed like a good enough plan for now, especially because I needed some money to pay for a place to live and for other things when I moved to New York. Attorney Lily told me that the prices for everything were higher there than in Hiawassee Springs.

I enrolled in my first classes since high school at the North Florida State University (NFSU). I had to get certain requirements out of the way before I could get deeper into the theatre program. I took an English class at Hiawassee Springs Community College (HSCC) for speakers of English as a Second Language to help my written English, taught by Professor Joshua Stone. He was tall and thin and kind and handsome and I did not notice a wedding ring on his hand. I had met too many married men who didn't wear wedding rings (at least not

ALL the time) in my previous line of work. Professor Stone seemed
available. I was interested in this man; that was for sure.

I stayed late after class to talk to him, and he told me he thought
my creative writing was good. He said that I had an "active imagination," and gave my "stories," which were mainly real stories about my
life, good grades. I thought he liked me, too. I wrote one story about
two women who live in an apartment together in a rural town in
Florida, one from Spain, and one from the Ukraine. The women
bond over their love of *telenovelas*. I guess the details were close
enough that he guessed that it was me, and the story seemed almost
identical to a story that Rosa had submitted. He asked me if I knew
Rosa. I told him that I did. He asked if he could drive me home that
day to discuss the story. I assumed he was after something more than
that. I was excited. I waited until we got into the car to suggest an al-
ternate itinerary. This was my chance to make a move. I couldn't very
well do it with Rosa around and I didn't have any privacy back at the
"shelter." Besides, I was embarrassed about sharing a room at the jail,
and didn't want Professor Stone to see where I lived.

"Why don't we go to your place instead, Professor Stone?" I gave
my blonde hair a toss and looked deep into his eyes, trying to show
him the things I wanted to do with him.

"Um, I don't think that's a good idea, Mila, especially since I was
hoping to talk with Rosa, too."

Stupid me, I had met too many men to get away with thinking that
any of them were good and kind. He wanted to have sex with both
of us! What a jerk!

"Why do you need Rosa, too, Professor Stone, aren't I enough for
you?" I asked, suddenly jealous. I tried my best to seduce him. He
gave an awkward and uncomfortable sounding laugh.

"Oh no Mila, it isn't like that at all. First of all, I am a happily married man. Second, I really like your writing. And Rosa's, too. I think
you guys have talent, and I wanted to suggest some ideas.... I didn't
mean to lead you on, Mila. I'm sorry." He looked down, sheepishly,
suddenly aware of what I thought. I was embarrassed, too. I followed
through to the end of the semester, but I never took another class
with Professor Stone.

Chapter 29

Lily

My clients are also Joshua's students. You have to love the 'wassee. After spending most of my life in big cities, I can't help but marvel at the coincidences of small town living. Bob Putnam may say that the community itself is dying, that the public sphere is eroding, that we must bowl alone, but no one in the 'wassee has received the message. Here, we bowl together.

Speaking of bowling, I had recently realized[55] that I might need a hobby. So, I searched around on my favorite Hiawassee websites and found that there is a group of women who meet up every other week to "Speak Spanish, enjoy activities, and discuss our common Latina heritage." "Perfect," I thought. I like spending time with women, I like "activities," and I am fully 50% Latina. Bring it on! I looked up the address and off I went to the local bowling alley to meet the other women. When I showed up, I realized that I was truly out of my league.

I walked into Rhonda Carter's Lanes & Fun at 8 p.m. on a Wednesday night, and sauntered over to the eating area, where the women said they were meeting. I looked around and saw only two groups of people. One included an unhappy looking woman, what must have been her grumpy looking husband, and their sullen child. Wow, no thanks. I looked around and saw a large group of loud women about thirty years my senior. I could actually hear them chatting away over the loud 80s rock playing.[56] As soon as they saw me walking in their direction, they all fell silent.

---

55. Well, maybe it wasn't exactly my revelation. Maybe it was more like Josh told me that I desperately needed to do something besides work and occasionally spend time with him. For him, work is both his job and his hobby; the joys of being a professional academic. For me, I had spent so many years in school and practice that I had lost track of what I might like to do "for fun." Fun was a tad alien to me at this point.

56. If you don't like John Mellencamp, you best go on home when it's 80s night at the Rock-N-Bowl.

"Jes?" One of them – who I later learned was Gloria from Honduras, a local acupuncturist – said, probably wondering why this crazy *gringa* was bothering her during her night out with the ladies.

I spoke in Spanish to the group of fourteen women, introduced myself as Lily, short for Liliana, and told them that my mother was from Argentina. They waited approximately three seconds before they started in on their favorite Argentinean jokes.

"How did the Argentinean commit suicide?" Gloria asked me. I actually had no idea, having never met more than a handful of Argentineans, and they were mostly family. "He jumped off his ego!" Gloria let loose an infectious laugh, followed quickly by the guffaws of the thirteen other women. I laughed, too, albeit awkwardly, because I didn't really get the joke. I had never been to Argentina, and in truth, I had never really identified as being part-Latina, given my translucent skin, reddish hair, and the fact that no one ever guessed that I was Hispanic. They told me that their group had been meeting for the last twenty years, each of them a transplant to the 'wassee from some other part of Central or Latin America. Get this, they call themselves *Las Chicas Horribles*.[57] In no time at all, I was one of those *"horrible"* women who, despite being more than three decades my senior, took me in like I was family.

It was helpful to meet with *Las Chicas*, and to spend time talking about something other than work. Both Rosa and Mila had decided that they were willing to help prosecute their traffickers, and so potential trials were in the works for both. Every day I was working with attorneys from the Justice Department and the FBI and preparing Rosa and Mila for what they would face in court. It was exhausting.

I didn't realize how very tired I must have been, and Josh, bless his

---

57. Apparently, around fifteen years ago, one of the former *chicas*, Lorena, wanted to head to her weekly meeting with her friends. Her husband was tired of the inattention bestowed upon him each Wednesday, and he asked her why she would choose to spend time with those *"chicas horribles"* instead of at home with him, where she belonged. Lorena left the house, and her husband, that night, and went to join her friends. She told the group the story, and from then on they liked to self-identify and reclaim the *horrible* in all of them.

heart, was too kind to ever say anything negative about my appearance. I appreciate the frankness of my clients who speak English as a second language, though, and not Spanish as their first. With them, we have no choice but to communicate with the English we can understand from each other, lots of hand signals and gestures, and many well-meaning smiles. Their honesty is just like that of children, who blurt out whatever feelings are on their mind at the moment. Like my niece, who, in the midst of a coloring project once told me, "Aunt Lily, I just farted. Daddy and I are very gassy people." It was definitely useful information, but probably something her adult father would not have shared. I digress. What I wanted to say is that one of my clients with limited English proficiency walked in the door last week, took one look at me and said, "Wow, Attorney Lily, you look so awful! You must be working very hard to look so bad!"

Huh. Not sure how to properly respond to that kind of abject honesty, and too tired to remember the details. All I remember is sharing that story with *Las Chicas* and hearing them roar with laughter. It was good to laugh again. Usually, the opportunities for humor in this kind of work are rare. Yesterday, I was preparing Rosa for how to deal with cross-examination by the Cuencas' defense counsel at trial. We had gone over their potential questions God knows how many times when she looked up at the wall behind my desk. My gaze followed her eyes as well.

"That girl, the one in the picture, she looks so much like me, don't you think?" Rosa gestured towards some public service announcement-like posters I had taped up to my wall.

Several different state and federal organizations had spent a good bit of money on creating a "Look Beneath The Surface" campaign to alert people to the dangers, and the existence, of human trafficking as modern-day slavery. The posters had about five different versions, one depicted a young darker-skinned boy washing dishes, another showed a young, possibly Hispanic teenager in handcuffs, looking despondent. Rosa was responding to a photo of a young girl's face, eyes cast downward. In truth, the little girl did look a great deal like Rosa probably had at age seven, with the same glorious hair. Still, Rosa's appearance – like mine, I suppose – had worn away a good bit since then.

What was funny about Rosa's comment? Well, I had distributed these posters all around the Southeastern United States, and sent them to community centers and churches all over the Panhandle for months. And nothing. I never heard of one person helped through my efforts. And yet, my client, someone already identified, labeled, and assisted as a victim of trafficking, could look at the poster, and without being able to see the writing from her vantage point, recognize something of herself in the sadness of that young girl.

"Yes, Rosita, I can see the resemblance." I smoothed down her shiny mane of thick, beautiful hair and fought back tears.

Chapter 30

Rosa

Hiawassee Springs, Florida
June 14, 2007

Dear Diary,

I wanted to have a great time at that dance with Philip Chan. Attorney Lily gave me a ride to Philip's house where we met his parents. They were very polite and nice, although they seemed surprised when I first walked in, and I realized that maybe Philip didn't tell them that I am Hispanic. I got the feeling that they might have preferred a nice Chinese girl for Philip instead of me. I was dressed up and looking my best, and when we were out of earshot of his parents, Philip told me that I looked pretty, and his face turned a deep crimson.

I wanted to have a great time at that dance, but I just couldn't. Philip's parents drove us to the high school gym, and promised to pick us up at 9:30, which was well before the dance was over, but Philip didn't seem the type to disobey his parents. He was so respectful, not like some of the other boys I had met in America. There was a band of musicians playing some nice music and so Philip and I started to dance, and I tried to imitate the other students, some of whom I recognized. Everyone looked so happy and alive, and I felt happy to be with them, dressed up and having a good time. After our fourth or fifth song I was starting to sweat and I was feeling really thirsty. Philip was also getting very hot and damp. He suggested that we break for a drink. We walked over to the table of sodas, water, punch and cookies. My eyes fixated on the punch. All of a sudden I was back at church, and Philip's sweet face looked like Marco instead. He filled a cup of punch and offered it in my direction. My hands were shaky, and as I dropped the cup of pink bubbly liquid, it splashed back across Philip's white pressed shirt. I tried to mumble an apology, but I started to cry, and I ran to the ladies bathroom, I locked myself in the stall, and I didn't leave for a long time.

I heard girls come into and out of the bathroom. Some of them stayed to smoke cigarettes, which we weren't allowed on school property, but I guess they felt safe hiding in the bathroom, blowing smoke out the window. I listened to their careless talk about boys and makeup and which teachers they thought were cute and who was dating who, and I desperately longed to be uncomplicated like them. I wanted to live in a home with parents like Philip's: nice strict Chinese parents who made you leave the dance early to get home at a reasonable time. I was shaken from my thoughts by the sound of my name.

"Rooooooosie! Rosie! Are you in heeeeere?" A voice I didn't recognize called my name like a song. That's what they called me at school, "Rosie." I wanted "Rosie" to be a different person than "Rosa." I wanted Rosie to be a nice American girl who went to dances and didn't throw punch on her date and hide in the bathroom for the rest of the dance.

"Rosie, if you're in here, Philip is outside the door and he is looking for you!"

I was so embarrassed, but poor Philip. I felt like I had to go back to the dance and at least offer a real apology. I got up off the cover of the toilet seat I had planted myself on who knows how long ago, unlocked the stall door, pressed the ladies' room door open and went back into the dance. There he was.

"I was worried about you, Rosie, are you okay?" Philip, still wearing his pink-splotched shirt appeared genuinely concerned.

"Oh, I'm fine," I replied, as if it were perfectly normal to spend hours in the bathroom when your date was alone at the dance. "I am very sorry about your shirt."

"I'm just glad you are okay, Rosie. I could always buy another shirt, but I could never find another Rosie." Philip's face turned the color of the punch, again, and I could see that the compliment was quite an effort for this shy boy. The music changed from fast to something more like a ballad. It reminded me of the songs my Papi used to sing to Maria and me when we were little.

"It is getting late, and I bet my parents are outside. Maybe one more dance?" Philip could tell that I was upset, and he tried his best smile, crooked teeth and all, and offered his hand. I felt terrible, after how the evening had gone, and much as I wanted to go back in that bathroom and never come out, I accepted his hand, put my hands around his shoulders like the other girls were doing, and his thin arms circled my waist. I looked around the room at all the other couples, tightly pressed together, some kissing, or looking straight into each other's eyes like they were in love.

"Thanks for coming to the dance with me, Rosie. I think you are really pretty." Philip closed his eyes and leaned toward me for a kiss. I quickly turned and gave him my right cheek. He didn't seem too disappointed. He smiled at me. I weakly smiled back. As the song ended, I looked over to the entrance of the gym, and could see Mrs. Chan. It was time to go. Thankfully, Attorney Lily was also waiting outside the dance, and she took me back to the shelter so Philip and his mom would not have to see where I was living.

Despite the punch incident, the dance was a nice distraction from all the other things I had on my mind. Even though they told me that the law said that I did not have to be involved with any of it anymore, I had agreed to help Officer Jim and the other attorneys and police put the Cuencas in prison. The police told me that the Cuencas were likely to go to jail for a long time for what they did to me and to Ana. Officer Jim and Attorney Lily assured me that Marco would get in trouble as well. It turned out that like me, Marco was not in the country on legal papers, so after he finished serving his time for making me do things with men for money and a drug charge he picked up for selling cocaine, he was going to be sent back to his family in Columbia.

Still, I was nervous. What if the Cuencas got out of jail and came after my family? They had always told me that they would come for Maria next, if I ever told on them. I had been a prostitute, and that is a crime. What if the police changed their mind and put me in jail, too, for violating the laws? Would Marco ever forgive me for turning him in? My feelings were very complicated. On one hand, I was frustrated with living in America, pretending to be a normal teenage girl named Rosie at school, and then going home to sleep in a shelter at night, talking with police and lawyers after school. That part of me wanted to go home to Jujuy more than anything. The other part of me wanted never to show my face in Jujuy again, not after the things that I had done. With men. It was all very humiliating. Also, if Señora Cuenca was able to find me once in Jujuy, she could find me again. She knows where Mami and Maria live, and I would not be able to protect them. Attorney Lily and Officer Jim told me that once the Cuencas and anyone else working for them are put behind bars, my mother and sister will be safer here in America, and Attorney Lily will get them visas to stay here legally and work.

I have not been able to find an option that seems simple. I long for the days when things were uncomplicated; when my biggest problem was my little sister Maria taking all the hot water from the shower, or hogging Papi's attention. Now, either I stay here and it's hard, or I go back, and that seems nearly impossible.

I miss my normal life, the life I had before, in Jujuy. For now, I have chosen to stay, and create a new "normal" here. I will face what comes next, and I will protect Maria and Mami, and hope for a better life for us here.

Chapter 31

Mila

I want to see Chico and his friends burn in hell. I figured the courtroom might be a good start. Attorney Lily and some other attorneys and policemen have been preparing me for my day in court, but I was born ready. Those assholes thought that they were going to have the last laugh, but boy were they wrong. I am going to take them down, and they will be sorry that they ever messed with Mila Gulej.

Attorney Lily was worried that I would feel upset about seeing Chico and Carlos again. It's true, I was a little scared. I mean, Carlos had found me before. How in the world had he found us? For months after Carlos had gotten us and made us work for him, I turned that one over and over in my head. Chico was savvy, but he wasn't that smart. It turned out that when Chico showed up to the VIP to pick me up the night that I left, the owner of the club, Sebastian, told him that I had taken off with Britney about half an hour before he got there. Chico was furious, but Sebastian calmed him down. He told Chico that he had taken down Britney's license plate a long time ago, in case any of us ever pulled any crap. Also, Sebastian had many friends who were police, given that he had met quite a few while running his little business operation in Atlanta for more than twenty years. More than a few cops owed him favors, and he cashed in on them for Chico. Chico knew that Britney had talked to me about going to Florida. I shared everything with Chico. Big mistake. So, Chico alerted his cousin Carlos who was just getting into the family business of trafficking in Florida. Carlos was in Jacksonville at the time, and all he had to do was to drive across the Panhandle, with the assistance of some officers, and find us at the Motel. Britney and I were no match for Carlos, Chico and their connections with the police.

Now, it is a different day. More than a year had passed since the day that Officer Jim found me, and I was ready to stand up and call Chico and his friends what they are: life stealers. Attorney Lily picked me up and drove me to the federal courthouse in Tallahassee and Judge Prinkle heard our case. The trial dragged on for a week. I had a different attorney representing me, but Attorney Lily stayed by my side as my immigration lawyer, and occasionally yelled "objection" and the judge would usually take her side. I got up on the stage and testified, I told the judge and the jury all the bad things that Chico and Carlos and Rodrigo had made Britney and me do. Chico and Jose were on trial for bringing me, and thirty-six other workers from Eastern Europe and Latin America to work in their Chinese restaurant, and Carlos was in trouble for being in on that scheme and the prostitution ring. Chico had managed to get a really good lawyer and he was trying to catch me in a lie, but I swore on that bible, even though I am not religious, that I would tell the whole truth and nothing but. So I did.

"Isn't it true, Ms. Gulej, that you decided to come to the U.S. to work in a restaurant, and that no one forced you to work there?" The defense attorney's sweat slid down his bald head, avoiding his long, slicked back black pony tail. I hated that look. If you are bald, fine, okay, but don't go growing a long pony tail like I am going to get tricked by all your hair down your back and imagine that there is something on top where there isn't. This Pony Tail lawyer was gross, and I didn't like the tone of voice he used with me.

"Well, yes," I said.

"And isn't it also true that you received special treatment at work because you were dating Hector Jimenez?" I didn't really know how to answer that question. "Hector" was Chico's real name. The way that awful lawyer looked at me, I couldn't tell if he was referring to the time I spent with Chico in the closet and how that time didn't count against my short break for the day, or something else. Before I could even answer it, my attorney got into the fray.

"Objection," said Mr. Price, my attorney from the government, as he stood and frowned at Chico's attorney. "Relevance?"

"Overruled," decided Judge Prinkle, "I want to see where this is going."

Mr. Pony Tail Lawyer continued, "And isn't it true that you are receiving a visa to stay in this country in exchange for your testimony in this case?"

What could I say to that? Yes, I was going to receive a visa, but I wanted to testify anyway. Would I have had the courage to testify against Chico and Carlos in court had it not been for the promise that I would get something out of it, too? I don't know. As I sat with the question, wrestling over in my mind how I would answer it, Attorney Lily was given permission to speak.

"Your honor," Attorney Lily said, "I have to object to this question. I'd like to take this time to educate the court about the T Visa." Judge Prinkle nodded his approval, encouraging her to continue. "The fact that Ms. Gulej may receive a T Visa as a certified victim of human trafficking is irrelevant to this trial. The United States Congress through federal legislation created a special right for victims of trafficking who cooperate with law enforcement to work and live in the United States. Ms. Gulej is not on trial here, and I would appreciate if Mr. Taylor would discontinue his line of questioning."

"Sustained," the judge said. The score was as follows: Attorney Lily, one, Mr. Taylor, zero. Go Attorney Lily.

"Mr. Taylor," Judge Prinkle continued, "will there be any more questions for Ms. Gulej?" Mr. Pony Tail Taylor said something about him not having more questions for me, but I didn't get down exactly what he said. At that moment, I caught Chico's eye, and he winked at me. The sight of that smile, and his orange jumpsuit made me queasy. My arms felt cold and bumpy and I felt like I might throw up. I focused my gaze instead on Attorney Lily, and her bright eyes and comforting smile felt like coming home. I decided not to be there for the rest of the trial, having done my part, and since no one had more questions for me, I waited it out in the shelter. Attorney Lily would come and tell me how it went each night.

My experience in court was slightly more traumatic than I had imagined, but it helped me make some decisions. First, everyone in that room was acting. I had never seen Attorney Lily be so formal, or frightening, really. She was really convincing in her performance. It got me thinking. I mean, I still wanted to be an actress, but I also want to destroy the people who have taken advantage of me, and Britney, and every other young person with a dream of becoming something great. I have decided that I want to be Erin Brockovich, looking sexy, but still making bad people pay for what they to do. I am almost done with my associate's degree at the community college and I'll start at NFSU in the fall. Attorney Lily suggested that I change my major from theatre to pre-law. I figure, it's all pretty much the same. By the time I'm finished, I'll be much older, and then either I'll take Attorney Lily's job, or I'll open up a legal practice with her, or maybe I'll be on the TV news as their legal correspondent. The sky is the limit for me.

There was just one more thing to do, to really move forward. I needed to connect with my past. My mother still had no idea of where I was, or anything that had happened. Attorney Lily told me that because I wasn't yet twenty-one years old, that I could actually petition for my mom to come to the States as well, and to start a new life here with me. I missed my mother so much, but I also knew that telling her about the visa would also mean I would have to tell her everything else, and I didn't want her thinking bad things about me. After weeks of mulling it over in my head, I decided to call, and to let her decide for herself whether she wanted to come join me. More than anything, I knew she would be so proud of me for deciding to continue with my education, and for that, I was proud of me as well.

I borrowed Attorney Lily's cell phone for the call, and she got a special phone card from the internet. We waited until almost midnight our time, so that I could be sure that my mother would be awake, and not yet out the door. I felt happy and like I might throw up at the same time. I pressed the glowing numbers on the phone, so many numbers for the calling card, and then the country code, the city code and the house number – it made my mother seem as far away from me in time and space as she was.

"Allo?" I heard my mother's voice in the phone, sleepy and startled at the same time. I took in a short, shallow breath at the sound of her voice.

"It's me, mama, it's Mila." I couldn't get another word out before the tears came, hers and mine.

Chapter 32

Lily

Josh and I are pregnant.[58] At first, I thought I might have a tapeworm, because I wanted to eat every two hours. After seven straight days and calling around for a good Gastroenterologist, Josh finally convinced me to buy a home pregnancy test and to see what's what. Well, turns out that it is in fact a human baby and not a tapeworm growing inside my belly.

Josh is thrilled. I want to be excited, too. I do. This baby deserves two parents who are completely excited that this little person is coming to live with them. I've said before, that I'm old enough for this phase of life, and lots of my friends and siblings have children. Still, it feels like some sort of anti-female conspiracy that just as I am reaching a high point in my career, a place where my work *matters* to people, and it *matters* to me, that I'm going to have to take a little time out.

I imagine that Josh wants to help, that maybe even he thinks he will be an equal partner, but I can already see how all of this is going to play out. He'll get wrapped up in his teaching and his writing, and well, he won't even hear the baby crying. We can't afford day care on our salaries, so one of us will need to be with the baby at all times. I just know that hypothetical "someone" is going to be me. But what about my clients? They are already here and their needs are immediate as well. Who is going to take care of them if I'm occupied with caring for a newborn? One I haven't even met yet?

I've heard from other people that a mom often feels like a mother from the second that she knows that she's pregnant, but that the father often doesn't slide into his role until the after the actual birth. In our case, the roles are reversed. Josh is overjoyed, and I am lukewarm about the whole situation. Maybe it would help if I could keep *any-*

---

58. I used to hate this term, the idea that "we" could be pregnant when it's my belly that protrudes out of my elastic-banded pants and my breakfast that hurls out of me each morning.

thing down right now. One minute I am absolutely ravenous, and the next I am sitting on the cold tile floor, hugging the toilet like it's my bestest friend.

So, there you have it, that's my latest news. I'm not the only one with news, though. For Mila, and Rosa, and I suppose me, our story is ongoing. Rosa is getting really frustrated because her mother and little sister are still waiting for passports from the Argentine government, and she has tried to be patient, but it seems like she doesn't quite understand why I can't just make it happen.

"You are an immigration lawyer, right *Abogada* Lily?" She asked, honestly, and without irony, also without making eye contact with me, clearly sheepish about asking the question.

I explained to her, for what feels like the hundredth gazillionth time. In reality, it is probably only the third time that she has ever asked, despite the fact that I'm sure her mother and sister ask her every time they call since they must be less patient, and perhaps less trusting of this so-called immigration lawyer who can't seem to bring them to the United States. I mean for God's sake, what is the hold up? Rosa is a child, she has been super cooperative, and she has long been certified by the police as a victim of trafficking. Derivative visas have already been processed and approved by immigration. So, why can't the U.S. government's left hand shake its right and have the State Department work with the Department of Homeland Security and just make this happen? It should be simple.

For whatever reason, it is infinitely harder to bring people legally to the U.S. than it is to send them back. Even though Rosa's family isn't yet here with her, and that is terribly unfair, she does have some things going for her. My friend Gloria (one of the *chicas horribles*), now an empty nester, has decided to join her daughter and son-in-law in Houston, but is going to keep her three-bedroom house as a "rental property." Basically, Gloria knew that the "shelter" was a problem situation, having been "evacuated" from her home during a turbulent marriage years ago when she spent some time living at the shelter, and she decided to help Rosa. She is charging next to nothing for rent, and Rosa's family will be able to eventually move in when they arrive. Whenever that might be.

I think I mentioned before that because Rosa was a minor, she was

not required to assist the police with the prosecution of her traffickers to receive the immigration relief. Still, she wanted to help. Rosa
gave her statements, but she was not required to come to court, much
to her relief. After much discussion, our team of attorneys and police decided that Rosa would suffer too much if she had to see the
Cuencas again. I went to their trial, though.

Sylvia Cuenca tried her best to convince the jury that she had
treated Ana and Rosa like her own daughters, but the truth came out
in the evidence. Some FBI agents had gone down to northern Argentina and discovered that the Cuencas were part of a larger ring of
local families who tricked young girls to come to the U.S. with them.
The criminals, many of whom were also originally from the impoverished towns, would show up in fancy clothes and jewelry, and give
the family some money, maybe even five or ten dollars to show that
they could spare the cash. The families, wanting the best for their
children, would happily send their children to the states, imagining
the great education and limitless opportunities they would have in
America, and excited that the children would send home some of
their copious earnings. No money ever did get sent back to those families. Some parents, or grandparents in Ana's case, never saw their
children again.

I wish I could say that Judge Prinkle put Sylvia and Jorge Cuenca
away for life, but because Jorge turned on his wife and confessed, he
will only serve a few years in jail, and his wife will spend five to ten,
depending on good behavior. If it is any consolation, their son Martin is going to do serious time for his crimes against Ana. Judge Prinkle found Martin guilty of both sexual battery and aggravated
manslaughter of a child. Together, the two offenses won Martin a
total of forty-five years in the slammer. Hopefully he will spend some
of those years thinking about what he did to Rosa's best friend.

Rosa is doing what she can to recover. She decided about a month
ago that she was willing to try therapy, and I finally found a Spanish-
speaking licensed clinical social worker willing to make time in her
packed schedule to see her. Rosita does think that her therapy is helping, but we have run into a new snag. The federal funding from HHS
will run out at the end of this month, and so we will begin the search
for some alternative ways to continue her much needed mental health

services. I just can't ask her therapist Cristina to work for free, although it may come to that since Rosa needs her help. Cristina's office is located in between a Pilates studio and a store that sells nothing but pictures of cats: I know that this town is culturally confusing for Rosa, but that is just one of many things we have in common. Each week, I take Rosa to her appointment with Cristina, and while they talk in private, I sit in the waiting room and write down our story. The writing process is my own kind of therapy.[59]

---

59. Our story could easily end here. The criminal court cases for Mila and Rosa are basically done, and they are on their way to recovering a sense of purpose for their lives, moving forward towards the future. Our story is different. It doesn't end at the moment that the do-gooder police force breaks down the brothel door, releasing the child sex slaves. It doesn't finish just because we are tired of hearing about the sad details of an exploited young person's life. Our story continues just as life continues, for all victims of trafficking who go on living. Sometimes, surviving day to day or even minute to minute is a challenge. The scars of trafficking might heal, but the wounds remain beneath the surface. Time moves forward, but things are messy and complicated. Our story could never be tied up in a neat package. Our story keeps going, long after you finish this book.

Chapter 33

Rosa

Hiawassee Springs, Florida
December 28, 2007

Dear Diary,

It has been so long that I fear I will never see Mama and Maria ever again. So much time has passed that Maria will be grown by the time they arrive. I am exaggerating, but really, why does this all take so long? I wonder if everyone at home forgotten about me? Do they miss me as much as I miss them? I wonder if they will ever find out about all of the bad things that I have done. I swear I would rather die than have them know. I wonder if Maria will be happy here in this strange new country. Will the kids make fun of her in school because she doesn't speak English? I will teach her all the English I know, and make sure that she signs up with a good teacher like Mr. Stone and that she learns really fast. She never did like school so much, but maybe she has changed a lot since I left. She was so small then.

And Mama, even though she is old, she'll have to learn as well. I mean, how will she know how to buy things in the grocery store if she can't ask people where to find the beans and rice or the parsley to make her chimichurri sauce for meat? How will she be able to know that people are charging her the right amount for vegetables or batteries if she can't count the money and know how to say the numbers in English? How will she be able to learn to drive? If we are going to make a life here, then Mami and Maria will have to learn to be Americans, just like I am learning. I think, if I can guide them, and help them, then maybe they won't find it so hard. I don't want it to be as hard for them as it was for me to be here.

It is Christmas vacation right now, a time I was looking forward to more than anything, to celebrate la Navidad with my family. They still aren't here. Attorney Lily is really nice and she must have known that this would be an especially tough time for me. So, she picked me up and took Mila and me to a local restaurant to celebrate. They had this really nice pine tree with silver and red tinsel sparkling sashes all over the tree, and lots of different colored shiny balls hanging from the branches. I could see my reflection in those balls, and I glowed different shades of gold, green, blue and silver. I looked strange to myself. Older, maybe, or just discolored.

Attorney Lily came without her husband, because she said he doesn't celebrate Christmas, so it was just the three of us girls, which made me miss Maria and Mami even more. I didn't understand what a lot of the food was on the menu, and I was feeling very overwhelmed. I could see the prices, though, and they looked very expensive, so I tried to order the least expensive item on the menu, whatever it was, and hoped it was something that I would enjoy eating. I pointed at something under the section labeled "Appetizers," and Attorney Lily looked surprised and asked me if I was sure that that was what I wanted, and that it would be enough. I assured her that it would; I really wasn't very hungry. It was kind of Attorney Lily to take us out and try to celebrate Christmas, but despite the nice tree and the fancy napkins and all of her best efforts at engaging us in conversation, I felt so far away from home, so removed from where I wanted and needed to be that it took everything I had not to just cry at that table. I held it in, though, so that Attorney Lily wouldn't feel bad about the really nice night she had tried to give us.

My small salad arrived and I could barely pick at it. The salad made me feel lonely. Still, not to be rude to Attorney Lily, I ate a few pieces of lettuce and some shredded carrots, thinking of the rich, warm food I would have had back in Jujuy. I looked around at the other patrons in the restaurant, some of them eating by themselves and wondered inside, "Who spends Christmas alone? Where are all of their families? What kind of a place is this where you go to a restaurant instead of eating in your home with all of your friends and family during the holidays?" I felt so sorry for those people in the restaurant, who may never have known what it was like to have a delicious, hot meal that you helped prepare for weeks in advance of the special day, all to share with friends and a big family. I glanced over at the tree again and saw that a red felt blanket had been placed under the tree to collect the pine needles and to put a few presents on. Except, there weren't any pine needles collecting because the tree was made of plastic. A fake tree.

I asked Attorney Lily who the presents were for, the ones under the tree, and she told me that they weren't real presents, but just empty boxes, wrapped up to look like actual gifts. I was so disappointed. What kind of a country was this with its cold meals in a restaurant on Christmas, its fake tree, its fake presents? I missed my real life, the one with real love, real affection, real family, real friends, real food, real presents and real trees. Attorney Lily must have seen how disappointed I looked and she reached into her bag and handed Mila and I each a box. I know it was a bit rude, but I shook to the box to see if it was empty like the ones under the tree, or if she had put something inside it. Mila opened hers faster than I could and exclaimed, "Cool, thanks Attorney Lily!" She ran to our lawyer and gave her a hug. Inside the box was a piece of paper for a gift certificate to a local store, where we could buy books, movies, or music. Again, the gift of more choices. Like that story I read in school where the clever boy realizes that he should wish for more wishes when he meets the genie in the lamp. I would have been satisfied with three. Sometimes it's just too many choices and I miss how simple things were in Jujuy, where I may not have realized it at the time, but I wanted what I had, and I had all that I wanted. It was nice of Attorney Lily, and I thanked her for dinner and the gift, and I wished her a very Merry Christmas. She looked pleased that we liked the gifts, and I was glad to have made her happy.

Attorney Lily drove us home, and I didn't feel much like talking. I was grateful to Mila for filling up the silence with talk of some movie that she heard about and how "hot" the movie star was playing the lead role and how she was going to star in a movie with him some day and I trailed off into my own thoughts. I know this is terrible, but I wished that it was Ana there with me, and not chatty Mila. Ana would have held my hand and waited for me till my family could come and join me. Ana would have made everything okay. I guess we had been parked for a minute or two before I realized because Mila seemed to be waiting, somewhat impatiently, for me to get out so that she could squeeze out of the right passenger door of Attorney Lily's two door car. "Goodnight, Rosa," Attorney Lily said, giving me a kiss on my right cheek, "Feliz Navidad." I wished her a Merry Christmas as well, and ducked out of the car and into the shelter where Mila and I still lived.

Wishing for more patience and faith to get me through this lonely time,

Rosa

Chapter 34

Mila

Mama and I talk often now. We set up a time to speak every Tuesday night, when she works until early in the morning and I can call her late in the evening, and with the time difference, we are both a little tired on opposite ends of the day, but hey, it's something. I still haven't told her much of what's happened with me since I got to the U.S. I can't bear for her to know that everything didn't turn out the way I had said it would. But we do talk, and I hear the same stories about the restaurant and the tourists and we laugh like old times. Maybe one day I'll tell mama everything, but I doubt it. I don't want her thinking about me like someone who is dirty, and I don't want her knowing the things her own daughter did.

Every time that mama and I talk she tries to get me to come home. I mean, I know mama misses me. I can hear it in her voice, and she outright says it. Still, I'm just not ready to face her yet. The thing is, I feel like I'm the one keeping mama and I apart. I really don't feel like I could face everyone back in Bratislava, but it turns out that I could bring mama here. Attorney Lily told me that there is this visa I can get to bring my mom here, and that she and I could be here together permanently. I know that's what Rosa wants, and well, good for her. But I'm not Rosa. I've done some horrible things that I'd rather not tell mama about or offer up to Jesus or whatever bullshit Rosa tells herself. She's a nice kid and all, but I'm not her. I have big dreams, and having my mom here would just get in the way all over again. Coming to America was my dream, not hers. She doesn't even want to be here and she would definitely try to drag me back to Bratislava and I'm not going. No way.

In the mean time, I am trying to build a life for myself here. Since I don't have any problem staying in America, at least not according to immigration, I figure why not just milk this place for all it's worth, right? It's been a rough road, but I have everything going for me: looks, intelligence, and talent. I am still trying to decide whether I want to leave this stupid small town and head to New York City or get some education before I go. Every day I wake up I feel like I want something different. For a little while I was really excited about becoming a lawyer like Attorney Lily. The thing is, though, it's just so many years of school, and by the time I'm done, I'll be as old as Attorney Lily. I can tell by looking in the mirror and by the looks I get from men that now I am at my best. Sure, it may last a few more years, but maybe I won't be this good looking forever, and then what? I need to have some serious money saved or a man to look after me or something. I really like art and make up and so I've also been thinking that instead of becoming a lawyer, maybe I'll become a cosmetologist and I can spend my days trying to make other people more beautiful. I mean, it could really help people around here who mainly don't wear any makeup or make any effort to look good, and it will be good to have this skill when I go to New York to become an actress so I can do my own makeup and they don't have to hire anyone special to make me look fantastic.

I've been practicing on myself with some cheap cosmetics I picked up from Walgreens. Lately I've been going out from time to time, just to feel like myself again. Last Friday night I got tired of listening to Rosa pray by her bed, so I got myself dressed up nice and I headed outside for a walk. I could hear live music from what sounded like somewhere to the left, so I followed Sharpe Street until I founded the origin of the music. It was live, and it sounded pretty good. There was a bouncer at the door, but I flashed him a big smile, tossed my hair and told him that I accidentally left my ID inside, but that I was a graduate student at the film school.

"Studying to be an actress, are 'yeh? Sure are pretty enough to be an actress...."

"Well, thanks," I said, giving the poor old guy a little wave and another big grin as I sauntered inside, already happy to have someone notice me again, even if it was a fat old man in Florida's version of Bratislava, small and irrelevant.

It was wood-paneled and poorly lit inside, but the band was playing blues and I liked it very much. I understood the blues. I looked around at the ten or so people in that bar, and I noticed most of them stealing glances at me. It's a small town, so it could be because they didn't recognize me, but it also might have been because I was looking really good. I noticed one guy in particular glance over at me three times before I nodded my head in his direction, and he decided to cross the room and join me at my table for four, with two chairs.

"What 'cha drinkin'?" The tall, somewhat good looking guy asked, comfortably falling into the rickety wooden chair he dragged from the opposite side of the table right next to me. I didn't have a drink in front of me, so it seemed like kind of a stupid question. It's not like I had so much money to spend, or anything, so I figured it was better that I didn't order a drink. I racked my brain to think of the drink that I most liked, the one that men at the VIP Club used to order for me.

"I'd love a vodka tonic, thanks," I said with supreme confidence and a big smile, making full eye contact with his wide-set blue eyes. "I'm Mila," I offered.

"Mila," he repeated, elongating the "eee" sound like a child on holiday in Europe told to say "cheese" for the camera. "That sure is a pretty name. Never heard it before. Spanish?"

Uninterested in explaining my story, and not sure this guy could tell the difference, I complied, "Yup, it's Spanish. My mom is from Spain." Once I started with a story, sometimes it was hard to stop. "From Madrid, actually. It's the capital. We can trace my mother's side of the family all the way back to—"

"I'm Ty," he cut me off with a laugh, "Ty Johnson. We can trace my family all the way back to the Panhandle for as long as any of us can remember, which ain't too long" he chuckled, clearly amused with himself.

I laughed along as well, taking a swig of my drink, pretending I got the joke. I brought my drink up to my lips with both hands, my tongue making circles, searching around for the thin, plastic straw. Finding it, I wrapped my lips around the small, red opening and sipped quickly until I made a slurping sound, having drained the cool glass of its contents.

"Woo hoo, Mila, good drink, yeah? Hey, buddy, she'd like another." Ty pushed a ten dollar bill across the sticky wood bar to the older man on the other side. Wordlessly, he obliged, sliding my next drink back down the bar to Ty. He caught it easily, with a well-worn hand, large and callused.

"Here you go, Mila, enjoy," he clicked against my glass with his beer bottle.

"Thanks," I said, already taking a few grateful sips of the drink, and wiping the cold wetness on the outside on my tight jeans with the back of my right hand.

Ty and I listened to the music, the band was blaring the blues, and I liked their sad, powerful sound.

"This music sucks," Ty said to me, leaning over into my ear, rolling his piercing blue eyes.

"Completely," I said, not thinking it sucked at all.

"You want to get out of here?" He asked, again into my ear, straining himself to be heard over the loud music.

I liked the music well enough, but was it that obvious? Of course I wanted to "get out of here." I wanted to be out of everywhere, out of my skin, out of Hiawassee Springs, out to anywhere but here.

Ty grabbed my hand, and directed me out of the club toward the parking lot. We walked over the gravel and my heart was racing. I was unsteady on my feet. Where would we go? Right then, I didn't care. I was happy to be heading somewhere.

Chapter 35

Lily

Mila is pregnant. That's right, pregnant. After all that I've tried to do for her, everything we have struggled for to help her move on with her life. She is pregnant. How could this happen? Why would she do this? Who's the father? I fired all of these questions and more at this child without any thought to the damage they might do.

"Attorney Lily, please calm down. This is a good thing. Ty is the father, I told you about him right? He's great, really nice, and not like Chico at all." Mila took my right hand in hers, gave it a comforting squeeze and locked eyes with me. She looked genuinely happy. She was obviously looking for some approval and I wished I could have just given it to her.

Oh great, Ty. Of course. Ty. Freakin' one syllable wrecking ball. Mila met him one night at the Cap'n Grille, this BBQ/fish/live music dive bar where the beer is cheap and the music isn't half bad. She isn't even old enough to drink legally, but the Cap'n doesn't mind, especially when you are as pretty as Mila. This guy kept feeding Mila drinks and bullshit about signing her for a modeling contract and the next thing you know, they are sleeping together. Turns out my grandma was right, it just takes one time, and boom, pregnant.[60]

I took Mila to the free clinic in Jacksonville to help her think through her options. I wasn't sure that she realized that she had any. Mila kept up her campaign of convincing the whole way there.

"Attorney Lily, this really is a great thing. I mean, I know that we had talked about me going to law school after I finish college, and I've been thinking a lot lately about heading to New York City instead, but Ty says that there is some local modeling and acting work that I could do here while we are saving up money to make the move to New York...."

---

60. Grandma, however, was not right about catching incurable skin diseases by using someone else's gloves, or at least, not in my experience.

On and on it went. Mila sounded completely convinced, and she did the best she could to persuade me, but I wasn't buying her version of the truth that would unfold over the next few years. So, Mr. Ty was going to answer all of Mila's prayers and help her accomplish all of her dreams? How was she going to be acting and modeling when she was 8 months pregnant? From Hiawassee Springs? Who was going to be watching the baby? Mila was a good talker, but not that good.

A few agonizing hours later of Mila trying to plead her case and me trying my best to sound convinced and supportive,[61] we got to the clinic. There were some great nurses at the clinic and they gave her all the information that exists on adoption or abortion, but Mila was not hearing any of it. For Mila, this baby is a tremendous gift and she could not be more excited to have what she is sure will be the little boy she has always wanted. Never mind that she still does not have a permanent place to live, almost no friends or connections in the States, let alone the 'wassee, is still in school and doesn't yet have a job to support her. Never mind any of that. Mila wants this baby, and nothing and no one can dissuade her. How could she have let this happen?

I know what you're thinking. I'm horrible. I should be encouraging Mila to do what makes her happy, or maybe I should stay the hell out of it. I'm her lawyer, not her mother, and I have totally transgressed the bounds of professional ethics. Still, I can't help but feel responsible. Okay, I didn't bring her to the U.S. and I didn't make her get involved with that Chico guy, but I have tried to guide her through every step of life since she broke free of that terrible situation. Maybe I feel bad because this is the first major event in her life since of all that shook out where she didn't seek out my counsel. Maybe this is my ego at play wondering why I'm not making the decisions for her anymore. If so, well, then shame on me. I'm here to be her advocate, not her boss, and not her mother. Mila has a mother she can talk to

---

61. You have to give me a little credit, right? I at least realized that no good would come from my sharing what I really thought about the whole situation with Mila. I kept my mouth shut. For me, a Herculean feat.

about this if she wants to. I just can't help but feel like she is messing up absolutely everything we've worked for.[62]

I hope this isn't what parenting feels like, because if it is, I am going to be terrible at it. I brought these concerns to Josh last week over dinner. Josh was rinsing off the lettuce – for the fifth time that night – to ensure that no bad organisms could possibly invade the perfect body of his unborn child growing inside me when I got home from the Jacksonville clinic with Mila.

"Hey babe, I'm in the kitchen," he called over the sound of running water as I walked in, and threw my purse on the couch and contemplated joining it. I was spent from my day with Mila.

Instead, I slumped into the kitchen and gave Josh a quick kiss on the cheek and he leaned in for a full on kiss on the mouth. I pulled away, in no mood for him. He stuck out his lower lip in a semi-mock pout, hair still rumpled from the rough day of an academic spent reading and writing from our couch. "What 'cha making?"

"I think dinner's going to be really good, sweetie. I've got Caesar salad going here with fresh homemade dressing, baked sweet potatoes in the oven, and some fish that I was about to sauté." Josh looked really proud of himself, like he just climbed an icy mountain in winter time instead of preparing a simple meal like I do for him every single night.

"What kind of fish?" I inquired, in full snark-mode, after a day of complete frustration.

"I got some tuna, the guy at the store said it was real fresh, and I was going to sear it in the pan, just like you like." He was trying his best, it was obvious, but I let loose on him anyway.

"Josh, have you forgotten that I'm eight weeks pregnant?"

"Um, no, of course not, honey. I think the way that you—" I cut him off before he had a second to respond.

"And did you know that there are certain foods I am not supposed to eat so as not to endanger the health of our beloved unborn child?"

---

62. And yes, I do realize that I sound like one of those stage moms who gets upset at her 5-year-old for putting on too much weight to win the annual Lil' Miss Hiwassee Springs pageant.

I picked up a spatula from our collection on the counter and pointed at him with it.

"I—" Again, no chance against Attorney Lily once she's gotten started.

"No, I guess you didn't. Because it's not like you would purposely feed me tuna and raw eggs when you know I can't eat it, right? It's not like you are trying to kill me, right? Why not make swordfish sashimi wraps with brie instead? God, what were you thinking?" I threw the spatula across the room and stormed off into the bathroom, slamming the door. My heart was pounding out of my chest and I waited a few minutes in silence for Josh to come after me. He didn't.

I started running the hot water, letting it warm up enough for a shower. It is hard enough taking care of a baby when they are still growing and protected in your body. How in the world was Mila going to take care of a baby on her own? I disrobed and got into the shower, looking down at my belly for any evidence of the baby. None yet.

Inhaling the nice, clean smell of the baby powder scented soap, I started to cry. Why was I acting like this? Frustrating day, no question, and I know that my hormones are all over the place. One thing kept nagging at me, though. Why was I taking it out on Josh? Was I really upset about Mila's baby or mine? She seemed much happier than me to be pregnant, so who am I to sit on my high horse and judge her decisions like I have all the answers? The tears kept coming, and my hands turned into little wrinkled raisins as I let the warm water wash my face clean.

Chapter 36

Rosa

Hiawassee Springs, Florida
February 13, 2008

Dear Diary,

I am still waiting. There isn't much else to say. Every week I pray that this will be the week that Mami and Maria finally come to live with me, but it never is. I hate this feeling, like my life is on hold until they come. I have prayed and prayed for an answer, something to mark the time, some way of showing progress, and then Jesus finally sent us a miracle. Mila is pregnant!

Mila is really excited about the baby, and so am I. She hasn't spent much time around babies, but I have, since my cousin Yesenia had her baby girl a few months before I came to America. I loved that little baby. I used to wash her, tickle her and dress her and she felt like this sweet little lump of sugar in my arms. I love a newborn baby – ooo, that sweet smell like powder. And I love the smell of that Menem soap that we would use to bathe her and smooth over her head of straight, black hair. Because Mila hasn't ever been around babies I promised to help her with absolutely everything, from holding her hand during childbirth and telling her when she needs to push or breathe to caring for her baby when she or he comes.

In the mean time, although things are going well for Mila, my life continues on, although without a huge, life changing event, like a baby, or the arrival of my family. I am in 9th grade now, what they call "Freshman year" at Hiawassee Springs High School, which seems like a strange thing to call it, since I am clearly not a man. I shouldn't be so surprised, since Spanish has lots of gendered words that also don't make much sense. Like, why is a map masculine? Why is a chemical feminine? The school year is going well and my grades from last semester were okay, nothing special. I was used to being such a good student that it is still hard to see anything but an A on my report card, but Attorney Lily keeps trying to remind me that my grades are very good given that English is my second language and that I basically just learned it. I can understand almost everything people say to me now, and I can communicate my thoughts and ideas, too. I am still as shy as I used to be in Jujuy, perhaps even more so, since I walk around feeling like I have a secret story that no one could ever guess, and that I would never want to share. I want to forget my secret story, and I never want to tell Mami or Maria or anyone at school. I want to forget, but I can't, since Ana is still gone, she'll always be gone, and one day I need to tell the world what happened to my best friend. I owe Ana at least that much, since she only came to America because of me.

Philip is in a few of my classes, and sometimes we sit together at lunch. Two shy immigrant kids making awkward conversation with each other for the allotted 40 minute period. It's no wonder that no one comes over to join us, despite the many empty seats at the table. I bet the other students would rather stand and eat their lunches than sit with us. Everyone thinks that he's my boyfriend, but he isn't. I don't think it would be appropriate for me to have a boyfriend that Mami hasn't met, especially since she is coming soon. I hope.

Certain things are different for me at school. I was always better at language and writing than anything else before I came here, but now I am good at math. I think it's because numbers are the same in Spanish and English, so before my English skills got as strong as they are now, Math is where I excelled. Anyway, I was asked by my math teacher,

Mrs. Lawson, to join this Math Club where we practice together for competitions all around the Panhandle area. Our group is called Mu Alpha Theta, which is actually a national group all around America. In my school, there are six of us, two girls and four boys and Philip is in the group as well. He is the smartest at everything, and math is no exception. We have our first competition of the year coming up, and Philip wanted to talk about it last week during lunch.

"Hey Rosie, are you nervous about the competition against Wakulla High next weekend? I heard they are really good." Philip never once looked up from his lunch while he spoke. He always ate the lunch Mrs. Chen packed for him in the same way: apple first, then carton of skim milk, then peanut-butter sandwich. He was a careful and precise eater.

"I guess, a little," I offered. In truth, I hadn't thought about it at all, other than during the Math club meetings. My thoughts were otherwise occupied by learning English, doing well in school, thinking of Ana, and bringing Mami and Maria here. I racked my brain for what a normal response would be and offered it.

"Actually, Philip, I think Wakulla will be strong competition for us. We should practice extra." I searched his face for some recognition of whether this sounded like something your average 9th grade math club member would say. Philip started to smile a bit, but then hid his smile with his right hand, pretending he was still swallowing a bite of his apple. I must have said the right thing.

"Well, Rosie, if you feel like you need some additional practice, then it's probably a good idea. Maybe you would like to come over to my house after school on Friday? My mom is a very good cook and she'll make dinner for us and we could run through some problems from the national workbook that Mrs. Lawson gave us ..." He trailed off, his face flush with the effort of his proposal. He was on to his skim milk *course by then and he finally looked up at me to see my reaction. I felt flushed as well, and I panicked. He didn't think that when I said that we need to practice more that I was suggesting something else? He must think I was being forward! I wasn't, though. How would I get out of this one?*

"Oh Philip, I can't this Friday, but maybe a different time?" As my voice rose with the question, I quickly got up, gathered my tray still filled with most of my uneaten school lunch and hurried to drop it off. Nice going "Rosie." I knew my reaction didn't seem normal at all. Maybe Philip didn't notice? Of course he noticed. He's so smart, and for all the English I can speak and the math problems I can do, I am still so far from the normal "Rosie" I'd like to be.

More soon,

Rosa

Chapter 37

Mila

How am I going to tell mama that I'm pregnant? I sat, staring at the phone, wondering how I would dial those numbers and spill the news. I don't think she will be excited for me at all, but we have this routine now, where I call every Tuesday night, and she relies on it, and well, I like talking with her, too. But it's Tuesday now, and it's time to call, and what the hell am I going to say? "Um, hi Mom, it's Mila. I'm pregnant." That will go over real big. I practiced ways to tell mama in front of the mirror, pretending like it was a movie about my life and that Lindsay Lohan was playing me. I got good at the flippant delivery, but not so good at the earnest one. I had about five minutes to go until show time.

I hate to admit it, but I have some mixed feelings about having this baby. For one, Ty is not in my life anymore. We saw each other a few times after that first night together, but he hasn't called me since I told him I was pregnant. That conversation really didn't go well. He said, "You are going to get rid of it, right Mila?" And I pretended like the connection went bad and that I couldn't hear him and I hung up the phone. He didn't try to call me back, and almost two weeks have passed since that conversation. Ty is 32 years old with what he said was a really good career and can't be bothered with my problems right now. I understand, I do. It's not like I had a dad around much when I was growing up, and I turned out fine. My baby will be fine, too.

The thing I am really worried about is what this baby is going to do to my looks. I mean, I have seen all of these awful pictures of pregnant women whose bellies were really stretched out and after, some of them had floppy skin and tits and well, how am I supposed to be an actress with a body like that? Ty had told me that there are some modeling jobs I could get in the area, so maybe they do pregnancy modeling, too, for those bigger clothes you have to wear during your last few months when the baby gets big inside you. I'm sure that even pregnant I'll be better looking than most non-pregnant people, so I should get those jobs, and then maybe I'll meet someone who could help me pay for reconstructive surgery to get my hotness back after I have this baby.

So, I'm not excited about being big and fat, and I don't really want to tell my mom that she's about to be a young grandmother, but there are so many other great things about having this baby. For one, I will never have to be alone again. I'll always have my little one to look after me when he gets older. I just know that I'm going to have a little boy, and I can teach him to be the kind of man that doesn't leave. He and I are going to be together forever. Now, time to call mama. I mustered up all the nerve I had and dialed. It rang.

"Hi my love," My mom's voice at the other end sounded tired and just the sound of her voice made my throat catch with the news I had to share with her.

"Hi Mama. I miss you. How is work going?" While she talked I racked my brain to decide whether I should tell. It was so much easier not to.

"Mila, are you still there? I'm talking to you." Mama sounded impatient. I wondered how long I had been lost in my own thoughts. Nevermind. Time to dive into some unpleasant water.

"Mama, I have something to tell you. I'm—"

"You're coming home! You are finally coming home! Oh Mila!" My mother started to cry, overwhelmed with excitement.

"No, mama, I am not coming home. Sorry. It is big news, though. I'm … I'm … I'm pregnant, mama." There it was, it was out there, hanging between us.

"Mila, no. No! How could you let this happen? Why couldn't you keep your legs closed, you stupid girl! You've ruined everything! I just can't …" I couldn't hear the rest of what mama had to say because she started to wail at the top of her lungs.

Although I felt like I had just been kicked right in the stomach, I still tried to talk to her. "Mama," I ventured, "Mama, please. This is hard enough …" I didn't have the chance to get out another word. The next thing I knew, the screaming, crying and cursing at the other end was replaced with an even more horrible sound: a long, steady, dial tone. My mother had hung up on me.

I patted my not-yet-protruding belly and spoke softly to my son. "It's just you and me now, little one."

Chapter 38

Lily

It seemed like a normal day at work yesterday. I was poking through some client files, when I started to feel like I had just gotten my period, which was weird, because your period stops when you're pregnant.[63] I went to the bathroom and noticed some bright red blood collecting in my underwear. I thought, "Stay calm, Lily, maybe this is no big deal." So, I got on the internet, and they said that some bleeding could be "spotting" which happens from time to time. I let it go for an hour or so, and just went back to my files. But I started to have really bad cramps, and when I went to the bathroom a second time, it looked like a blood clot the size of a golf ball. I started freaking out and called Josh. Cell phone, office line and home phone — nothing. I left some panicky messages where I tried to sound calm, cool and collected, but I doubt I would have fooled anyone.

"Hi babe, it's me. Um, I'm not feeling well and I think I might need some medical attention. Call me back when you get this?" So went the first message on his cell. By the third message I had to leave without finding Josh available it sounded more like, "Josh, pick up the Goddamn phone! I'm dying and I need you, where the f**k are you right now???" Okay, so I certainly would not have fooled anyone at all. But where was he when I most needed him? Writing the next great American novel, for Pete's sake? Answer the phone, Josh!

I called my obstetrician's office, Dr. Curly. Dr. Curly had delivered just about every last baby in town … since 1963. I trusted him completely, even though he was hard of hearing and almost always with another patient (or out fishing). I dialed and the nurse practitioner picked up.

"Dr. Curly's office, Mandy speaking." She drawled.

---

63. I don't mean to be Captain Obvious, but some of this common sense stuff they just don't teach you in school.

"Hi nurse Mandy, this is Lily Walker Stone, I've got a prob—"

"Well hey there, Lily, how in the world are you doin'? How's that handsome husband of yours? What a gorgeous little baby you are going to have between those beautiful curls of yours and his trim body, my word! Well, it's delightful to hear from you, but we aren't due to see you for another few weeks—"

"I know, nurse Mandy, but that's why I'm calling. I've got some bleeding going on, and it's heavy, and I'm worried." I tried my best to remain calm, but I could feel my thin linen pants getting increasingly damp.

"Oh goodness, well, Dr. Curly won't be in the office for another few hours, but if it's a true emergency ..."

"Nurse Mandy, this *is* a true emergency. Please. I'm scared." There, I said it. In a rare bout of honesty and ability to articulate my needs, I put it all on the table.

"Okay, sugar. If you feel well enough to drive, then get yourself to the office and I'll see you right this instant."

I left my files scattered on my chair and drove the twenty minutes to Dr. Curly's office. I looked down and saw that a red blotch had crept across my light grey pants, staining the front and back. Growing faint at the sight of my own blood,[64] I tried to focus and drive faster. By the time I arrived, I was feeling woozy. It took all the strength I had to enter the office, signal to nurse Mandy that I was there, and collapse into a chair in the waiting room.

The next thing I knew, Mandy was standing over me, along with some medical-looking people, and they were driving me to the closest hospital. I tried to talk, but I could barely get any words out, and Mandy stroked the sides of my face and tried to sooth me.

I next came to in the hospital. I was wearing one of those scandalous hospital gowns that leave your backside exposed and I had all kinds of tubes stuck into my arms. One tube fed me a clear looking

---

64. It's true. In my family, you either become a lawyer or a doctor, and well, I knew right around 7th grade when I refused to dissect Skippy (the frog I had named and befriended in Biology class), but was able to construct solid arguments as to why the dissection practice was barbaric and refused to participate that I was likely to end up in the lawyer camp of the Walkers.

liquid, and another looked like blood. I should have been more freaked out, but I felt too exhausted to think straight. As soon as I could open my eyes and get them into focus, I saw Josh's face. He looked so worried, and I didn't know how to react, so I turned away.

"Lilybillygoat," Josh put his face inches away from mine. His breath smelled sour, like he hadn't eaten in a long time. "You okay? I was so worried. I'm so sorry I wasn't there …" His voice trailed off and he pulled up a chair next to my bed, burying his face in his hands, and sobbing.

"Josh, ssssokay," I slurred, trying to smooth down his tousled hair, but I had limited mobility since I was attached to an IV. Given my inability to talk, they must have had me on some kind of strong medication.

"That's right, Lily, everything is okay." It sounded like he was trying to reassure himself more than me. "Everything is going to be fine…" He started crying again, trying to hide his tears in his hands.

"Josh … am I going to be okay?" I started to worry as well. He nodded yes, but he still seemed so upset.

"Josh, what about the baby?" We locked eyes, and the tears started flowing, his and mine, and they just didn't stop.

"Lily …" Josh didn't even have to say it … I just knew.

"What did I do? I'm so sorry, Josh." I plead with guilty eyes. He stood up and smoothed my damp hair back from my sticky forehead, wet with brushed away tears and sweat.

"Lilybillygirl, you are the best. It's not your fault. The doctor said that you need your rest now. Let me let you sleep." I reached for his hand but he slipped it out from under mine, and turned his wet face away, still trying in vain to cover it with one arm, and walked out the door.

"Joshy, please don't go. I need you …" I trailed off. I wanted to follow him out the door, but I was too groggy to move.

Chapter 39

Rosa

Dear Diary,

Since I got to America, so many of the days have blended together. Even ones that used to be special to me, like Christmas and my birthday, either seemed unimportant to everyone here, or like they were celebrated all wrong. Today is better than Christmas and my birthday combined: Mami and Maria are here—they are finally here!!!! In Hiawassee Springs!!!

Just when I was finally starting to give up on Attorney Lily, she got an envelope from the United States Citizenship and Immigration Services about a month ago and the letter inside granted the visas for my family because of everything that happened to me. I expected it to have some sort of explanation for why everything took so long, but it was a thin envelope and it didn't, and it doesn't really matter anyway because the letter had the word "APPROVED" written under where it said Maria Lucia Hernandez, minor sister, and Isabel Esmeralda Hernandez, mother. Their names looked odd to me, typed onto a congested page with formal writing in English. It was odd and beautiful to finally see my beloved Mami and Maria acknowledged by the American government as official, officially on their way to be with me again.

I read the letter probably ten times, just to make sure that it was real, that my family was really, finally coming to be with me. Attorney Lily asked me if I was ready for them to come. Was she kidding?

"Now Rosa, I know that you have been waiting a long time for this, but having your family here will be a big change for you. You will be moving into a different house, away from Mila, and your family will rely on you to explain everything about the U.S."

"Ya lo se, Abogada Lily." Yes, I know this. I tried to appear patient, but I really wanted her to get to the part where she told me exactly when they were coming and where I would meet them. Attorney Lily didn't get my clues, which might have only happened inside of my head, since I was outwardly more respectful and patient than I felt on the inside. She continued on.

"Also, they might have more questions, like about why they were allowed to come be with you in the U.S. I just want you to know that you don't have to tell them anything you don't want to, okay?" Attorney Lily pressed her hands over her desk and looked earnestly into my eyes. I tried not to be annoyed with her, since I know she means well, but we are talking about my family. I knew what I would tell them and what I would need to keep from them to protect their idea of me as a good, Catholic girl. And so I let Attorney Lily continue on with her explanations of why having my family with me might be difficult, and I tried to nod and look concerned or smile at the right times, but my heart was leaping out of my chest with excitement. They were finally coming!!!

Attorney Lily explained to me how the state department secured their visas with the department of the homeland security, which apparently handled a lot of immigration matters, but the details weren't so important to me, other than the information that was going to tell me exactly when they were coming so I could start counting down the hours, the minutes, the seconds until I saw them again.

After what seemed like forever and a day, Attorney Lily told me that they would arrive in the capital city of Tallahassee at 10:45 a.m. on Delta Flight 2559 from Atlanta, previously from Buenos Aires, Ar-

gentina (where Attorney Lily was originally from, and the capital of
where I used to live). I had heard some things about Atlanta as well
from Mila, and I was concerned.

"Abogada Lily, um, how much time will they spend in Atlanta?" I
tried to appear casual with my question, but I think Attorney Lily
could see the worry crinkle that sometimes appeared over my left eye
when I was especially concerned about something.

"Rosa, please don't worry," she said, gently squeezing my hands
again over her metal desk, "They only have a layover long enough to
get through customs and to catch their next flight." Phew. I wanted to
believe Attorney Lily, because it made me feel so relieved.

She was right. Someone from the airline helped Mami and Maria
call Attorney Lily's phone from Atlanta, and they also made sure that
they got on the flight to Tallahassee. After we heard their call, Attorney Lily and I started the drive to Tallahassee Regional Airport to
make sure that we were standing there, flowers and signs in hand,
waiting for them when they walked through the gate. It was their
first time on a plane, and as I thought about their journey, and heard
the nervousness and excitement in their voices when they called to
check in from Atlanta, I thought about my similar trip with Ana.
Everything has changed for me, but has it changed for Maria and
Mami as well? Maria must be so big now, almost the age I was when
I left. The very thought gave me shudders. Maria is just a little girl.
She will need a lot of protection here.

Attorney Lily and I talked part of the way from Hiawassee Springs
to Tallahassee, but I could not keep my head in the conversation. I
kept thinking about Mami and Maria, and Ana. Even though the ra-
tional part of me knew that Ana wasn't coming with them, it still felt
like home was coming to me, and Ana had been part of home for as
long as I could remember.

"Rosa? Rosa? Earth to Rosa . . . " Attorney Lily was apparently trying to get my attention for some time, but I hadn't even noticed, until she gave my shoulder a playful nudge. "You doing okay, mi amor?" Attorney Lily seemed genuinely concerned, trying to make eye contact with me while maintaining minimal – but safe – contact with the one-lane road that lay in front of us, huge green trees from the Apalachicola National Forest lining either side.

"Oh yeah, good, yeah," I replied, still lost in my thoughts about Ana and completely distracted. I was feeling good, I think, but I was so excited that I was also starting to feel queasy as well, like I might vomit. I felt myself actually turning green. "Um, maybe not so . . . Lily pull over, please . . . " Attorney Lily started to pull over onto the gravel and grass and I barely made it in time to open my door and heave out the side. Attorney Lily was next to me in an instant.

"I thought you looked a little queasy, pobrecita," she rubbed my back in gentle, soothing circles while trying to give me space. "Aw, mi pobrecita," she repeated, continuing with the back circles while I threw up everything I had managed to get down that day. What had gotten into me? Was I sick? I took a few deep breaths of the increasingly warm late spring air which calmed my acidy stomach. I just could not believe, after everything that had happened, that they were finally coming to be with me. It was so much to take in.

The next hour flashed by and the next thing I knew, Attorney Lily and I were waiting next to the gate and the computer screen said that their flight had arrived. I had made a sign with their names on it, like I was a limousine driver waiting on some important clients, and I held it up, searching the trickle of passengers emerging from the gate area for their faces.

Then, all of a sudden, I saw them. Mami and Maria, brown and beautiful, looking lost and nervous and I ran to them, my paper sign bearing their names crushed in the middle as I wrapped my arms around Mami. The three Hernandez women, together at last! I never wanted to let go.

Grateful and happy again,
Rosa

Chapter 40

Mila

I was with my son in the desert, drowning in quicksand, and Mama stood over us, laughing, shaking her head and saying, "You could have been someone, Mila. Why would you do this to me?" As she spoke these hateful words, she bent over and pushed my head further towards the sand.

I was pleading with her to save us, to save her grandson at least when a bell sounded. I woke up, and as soon as I got my wits about me, I answered the phone.

"Hello?" I croaked into the receiver, barely awake. It was Attorney Lily.

"Hi, Mila. I'm coming over. You ready to be picked up in ten minutes or so?" Attorney Lily sounded impatient, which wasn't really like her.

"Uh yeah, ten minutes, no problem. See you then." I bolted out of bed and threw on some clothes, wrinkling my nose at how my purple T-shirt seemed unnaturally short and tight around my expanding stomach. "You are causing all kinds of problems already, little one," I said disapprovingly to my belly. Within minutes, I could hear Attorney Lily outside with our agreed upon honk, two long, one short, and another two long honks. I threw my keys in my purse and bolted out the door.

I opened the door and hopped in, giving Attorney Lily a quick hug before I put my seatbelt on.

"You're late, Mila. This wasn't an easy appointment to get." Attorney Lily was in quite the mood. Well, too bad. I had things on my mind, too. What did she have to be unhappy about anyway, with her perfect man and her perfect job, her perfect life? I bet her mother approved of all of her choices.

"Sorry, overslept," I mumbled, looking straight ahead, not interested in making eye contact with my cranky lawyer.

We drove most of the way in silence, but luckily the doctor was pretty close by. It wasn't close enough for me to walk, and this town has really bad public transportation, so there wasn't even a bus I could take. I wasn't ungrateful for the ride from Attorney Lily, but she didn't have to be rude about it, right?

We went into the doctor's office, Attorney Lily gave the ladies behind the desk my name and she helped me fill out some papers attached to a clipboard. I looked at the lines that asked for my family health history, on my mom's side, and then my dad's. I had no idea about any of it. My dad seemed healthy enough, the few times I ever saw him, and it's not like I could call my mother now and ask about any diseases or anything on her side since she didn't seem too excited about talking to her only daughter. I had to leave a lot of the form blank and hoped that later on, mama and I could talk again and I could find out the answers to all of this stuff.

"Ms. Goo-lodge, Meye-lah Goo-lidge?" I heard my name butchered by one of the nurses calling it, and the way she pronounced it, like I was some kind of unusual disease, made me feel even farther away from home.

"That's us," I said to Attorney Lily, as I got out of my squishy leather chair.

"Okay, Mila, good luck," Attorney Lily gave me a reassuring smile and then went back to reading some fashion magazine she seemed very interested in.

"Aren't you going to come with me?" I asked, trying not to sound desperate, but I just assumed that she would come with me. So, she was just my ride now and that was it? I didn't want to do this alone.

"Oh, sorry, Mila, did you want me to?" Why in the world would she think I would want to do this alone? Attorney Lily sounded strange and vaguely far away to me. Why was she making me beg like this? Fine, Lily, fine. Here you go.

"Um, yes. Thanks. That would be great. Please?" I threw her a plaintive look and tossed my long, blonde hair. That move usually worked with men to get me what I wanted, but I had never tried it on a straight woman before.

Attorney Lily smiled, put down her magazine, got up from her chair, and walked with me past the open door, following the nurse to the back room areas.

The nurse, Libbie, made me pee into a cup and write my name on the outside label with a black marker. She took my blood pressure and asked me questions about whether I was feeling nauseous, tired, swollen or having bad headaches. I told her that I had thrown up a couple of times, which was true, but the baby only caused part of that; I think the other part happened because I hated seeing all that extra weight in globs all over my body. I didn't think Libbie needed to know that I was feeling bad about my body, and Attorney Lily didn't need to know either, for that matter.

After I told Libbie everything she needed to hear, she took me to another room, covered in awful lime green wallpaper with a dark green ivy print climbing the walls. She had me switch into a gown like they wear in hospitals and Attorney Lily thankfully picked up a magazine from the bin on the door and didn't look at my fat pregnant body while I changed out of my clothes.

A dark skinned woman entered the room a few minutes later and introduced herself.

"Hi, Mila, I'm Veronica. I'll be doing your ultrasound for you." She seemed nice enough, but she pronounced my name like it rhymed with vanilla, which I found pretty annoying. I tried correcting her the nicest way I knew how, but I was nervous. What is an ultrasound and why did I need one?

"Hi Veronica. I'm Mila, and this is Att—" Attorney Lily stuck out her hand to Veronica and introduced herself, "I'm Lily." There was no sense in disclosing that the "friend" who had come with me to my appointment was actually my lawyer. I don't know why, but I found it embarrassing that the person who came with me was my attorney, like I didn't have any real friends but I had to pay her for her time or something, as if sitting in a hospital gown in front of a total stranger wasn't bad enough.

"Well, pleased to meet you both," Veronica said kindly. "Ready to check out your baby, Mila?" She made a point of pronouncing my name correctly that time. I decided I could try to like her. Veronica squeezed some cold blue gel out of a tube that looked like the one my mother used to use to decorate my birthday cakes on those rare years we could actually afford one. I think I had last seen one for my eleventh birthday. The frosting was pink, butter cream and delicious.

"Mila?" Veronica said my name. "Where are you girl? Take a look at the monitor." I turned my head towards Veronica and saw a big black screen with some grey and white smaller images moving around. "That's her foot right there. And there's her little leg. Can you see?" Veronica moved the joystick looking pen around the outside of my stomach, very excited at the images within. I really didn't think they looked like feet or legs or anything but a little mass of mush, and why was she calling my little boy "she"?

"Um, Veronica, can you tell what my baby is yet?" I asked, nervous, already anticipating an answer I wasn't quite sure I could handle.

"Why yes, sugar, it's a beautiful baby girl!" Veronica spilled over with excitement and I almost threw up all over her. I couldn't manage to make even a sound.

Attorney Lily said what I guess the appropriate response might have been, "Wow, that's so exciting," but her voice also sounded devoid of excitement and my head was already spinning with the idea of a girl. What was the point of having a girl? I wanted a boy, a son to love and protect me. Life is too hard for us girls. I didn't want to be bringing another one into the world to be hurt, kicked around, and left.

Veronica checked the baby's heart, searched the face for problems with the mouth, made sure the organs looked good and then wiped the blue goop off my stomach. Attorney Lily helped me pay the bill given all the insurance issues and then she found a time when she was free to drive me for my next appointment. I had to come back every month to have them look at the baby. I felt sick and I didn't want to go back to that office, no matter how nice Veronica was, I would still think of her as the one who told me the baby isn't a boy. How could this have happened?

Attorney Lily dropped me off at the shelter, I went straight to my bed without removing my shoes, and just started to cry. It's not fair. After everything bad that happened to me, all I wanted was a little boy to love and one day, a grown up son to love me. Now, there is a girl inside me, giving me a fat belly and flabby arms, stealing my good looks, and making me feel sick. I didn't want any part of this.

I whipped out my phone and called my mother. The phone rang

a few times, but she didn't pick up. Where was she? I tried calling Ty. Even though I hadn't heard from him in practically forever, I thought maybe we could meet up for a drink, and take my mind off of things for a while.

The phone rang twice and he picked up.

"Yello," I felt happy at the sound of his deep voice at the other end. I tried to appear nonchalant.

"Oh hey, Ty, it's Mila." It seemed pretty convincing, except there was dead silence at the other end. "You there, Ty? I said, it's Mila." I tried enunciating, thinking maybe my accent made me hard to understand.

"Hey Mila. Um, what's up?" Ty sounded confused, like he couldn't figure out why I called or who I was. I was getting annoyed and decided to clarify it for him.

"Well, Ty, I just came from the doctor, the OB-G—" Ty cut me off before I could even tell him that he was about to be a father to a little girl. I could hear the sound of a woman giggling in the background. "Who's that?" I demanded. "Ty, I am trying to—"

"Hey Mila, it's, um, real great to hear from you, but I'm really busy right now, between work, and" more giggling in the background, "Hey, stop that! Stop!" there was more laughing, "Anyways, I really gots to go." The dial tone rang into my ear. I couldn't believe that he hung up on me. Just like that. I couldn't take it anymore. I grabbed the bottle of coconut flavored rum that Ty had given me as a present the last time we got together and probably made the baby and started drinking straight from the bottle. "Wouldya like a drink, Mila?" I tried to imitate Ty's drawl. "Why yes, thank you, Ty, that would be great." I took a swig of the imaginarily offered rum. I didn't want to be awake anymore, and I didn't want to think about the baby girl inside me who would ruin my life, and her own one day. Like mother, like daughter.

Chapter 41

Lily

We lost the baby. Josh and I. It's all over. I never knew I could be so sad about losing something I wasn't sure I wanted in the first place. Josh and I were going to wait until I was 12 weeks along to tell everyone, and well, now there is nothing to tell. What do you do at this point? Call up your mom and say, "Yeah, I am feeling sad because I had a miscarriage, and they had to remove part of my uterus and now I can never get pregnant again." I can only imagine how that conversation would go?

"You are pregnant????" My mom would squeal into the receiver, incredulously happy, always half listening and looking for the most optimistic information.

"No, mama, I was pregnant, but we lost the baby, and I'm sad." I would try to say it patiently, but my sadness would overwhelm me, and she would hear the anger in my voice.

"Oh, I see. Well, you can just try again! Trying can be lots of fun!" I would feel simultaneously softened and embittered by her desire to gloss over the details in the interest of moving on, and I would make some excuse about a client needing some help and I'd get off the phone quickly.

As you can see, I can't call my mother, and it has been so long since I've called any other friends, having spoken to people sporadically since I met Josh and we moved here. I don't have any new friends here that I feel close enough with to talk to about this sadness, and my old friends finally stopped trying to get in touch with me more than a few months ago.[65]

---

65. And who could blame them? Between feeling wrapped up in my clients' situations and trying to ignore my marriage going down the tubes, I didn't much feel like volunteering information with anyone. I suppose I could have called *las chicas horribles*, but I was remiss in even getting in touch with the group of women I had joined for fun. I was feeling lower than low.

Losing a baby and knowing that I can never have another: well, these things would be hard enough to manage. Lately, I am feeling worse, mainly because no one knows what I am going through, and Mila's pregnancy requires my involvement, since she doesn't drive and she needs some help and guidance through the process. I wish I could say that I have been offering this assistance with an open heart, but I feel so annoyed at her, for the ease with which she got pregnant, her ability to have as many kids as she would like, and the fact that she doesn't seem to want the child now that it's a girl and not a boy. Unbelievable!

I've tried to talk to Josh about all of this, and it's really not going well. He thinks that I have way overstepped my boundaries with my clients, and that I'm no longer their attorney but also their mental health specialist, their driver, their translator, and on and on. It's not that he's wrong, it's just that I feel there isn't anyone else to plug the gaps that remain in their lives, or in mine for that matter. These gaping holes are turning into larger chasms by the day. My life with Josh is no exception. We fight, always over something stupid, when it's clearly the underlying issues that are really the problem. For example, the latest explosion that occurred about two days ago went a little like this.

"Hey Lily, whacha want for dinner tonight? I'm thinkin' spaghetti." Josh yelled from the kitchen, already boiling water and opening a can of crushed tomatoes for the pasta sauce.

"Why does he even bother asking me when he's already making what he wants?" I grumbled out loud, half to myself.

"Hey Lily, spaghetti okay?" Josh sounded a little annoyed, maybe because I didn't answer him, or possibly because he was tired of making dinner. I just wasn't feeling up to cooking or standing on my feet more than necessary since the partial hysterectomy. My doctor said that I was physically healed by now, but still.

"Yeeeeessss!" I screamed back into the kitchen, a little louder than necessary, wondering why I had to respond at all, since clearly we were eating spaghetti whether I wanted to or not. There was no response from the kitchen, or maybe there was, because twenty minutes later I heard Josh pour the pasta into the colander and then onto two plates. By the time I got myself up to walk over to the kitchen, Josh was already eating.

"Would it have killed you to wait for me?" I sulked as I nibbled on the spaghetti, swirling it around my folk, watching it fall down, and then catching it on my fork again.

"Sorry," Josh said, not sounding for a second like he meant it. The rest of the meal passed in silence, and then Josh went to clean up.

"Let me help you," I said, getting up from my chair with my plate.

"Don't bother," Josh retorted, "I wouldn't want to put you out," and grabbed my plate from my hands so hard and so suddenly that it dropped to the floor, a piece of the jagged green ceramic landing near my bare foot.

"Great, I could have cut myself," I said, accusingly to Josh.

"Goddamit, Lily. Not everything is my fault." Josh stared straight at me. His normally erect shoulders slumped. He paused for a good long while. "I can't do this anymore."

Do what? Make dinner? Be married to me? At that moment, I didn't really care. Fine. Josh was tired of me now? Now that I couldn't give him the children he always wanted, maybe he'd like to run off with one of his students. Well, fine, I didn't need to stay with him in this crappy cretin-infested house with his bad cooking and his monosyllabic interactions.

"You can't, Josh? Well neither can I. Maybe I'll head back to D.C., spend some time with my family." There was ice in my voice, and I had steeled my spirit against whatever emotional arsenal he was about to throw my way. We had had at least thirty conversations just like this one in the past month, and I was fed up. What in the world was I doing here anyway? I needed some time away. I waited for his response, the part where he begs me to stay, to share our life together in this small town. It didn't come.

"That sounds like a good idea," he replied, without sarcasm or sadness.

"Fine," I said, and left the room, searching the house for a place I could be alone. Finding nothing but the bathroom, I closed the cover on the toilet and sat there for a while. I thought that Josh would fight for me, for us, but maybe I'd pushed him far enough away that he was tired of fighting.[66] I'm certainly tired of fighting with him. Sure, I'd thought about leaving several times in the last two years, but not in any concrete way. Rosa still needs me, and much as she is driving me nuts, I believe that Mila does as well. They aren't the only women who could use my help, though. Human trafficking and other exploitation of immigrants is a problem in many parts of the U.S., and the world. I could go stay with my mom's sister Claudia in Buenos Aires and do some work there, or look for jobs back in D.C.

I walked out of the bathroom and into our shared bedroom. Josh was in the process of taking a few books and blankets out of the room.

"Hey, where you goin' with that?" I asked, half curious, but mainly to try a conversation with Josh that wasn't tinged with anger, resentment and pain. It was my best attempt.

"The couch," he said, over his shoulder, without making eye contact with me. I guess he was right. If I couldn't help make him a child, then no point in "trying" anymore. I let him walk right out. I took a deep breath and slowly exhaled. If Josh was no longer going to be my compass in this crazy world, I would need a new direction. The idea of him leaving was more disorienting than sad, which in itself is a terribly sad thing to say. Did I even love him anymore, or did I just love the idea of being attached to something, knowing that I was moving in one particular direction? The only word for what I felt was in Spanish. I felt "*desubicada.*" Lost, but not just disoriented. I was lost without a clear idea of where I might be headed.

---

66. Maybe he never wanted to fight for me in the first place. I might have made things too easy for Josh. I mean, he never really had to win my love. Everything for us happened so quickly, like insta-love. Now, it felt like it was falling apart just as quickly, like pliable strands of string cheese, and maybe that's because we built love like a house of cards, no support, pulled away from our support systems, we just couldn't make it work for each other. We weren't strong enough. Knowing we weren't going to be parents, there just didn't seem to be a reason to stick it out anymore.

Chapter 42

Rosa

Dear Diary,

I'm so sorry that it has taken me such a long time to write, but it has been a very busy time. I had waited and wished and wanted for Mami, Maria and me to be together for so long. I imagined what it would be like, how I would show them around, teach them English, and ease them into all of the weird things that make America different from our country. They have now been here for six months, and while it is the most wonderful thing for us all to be together, at last, it isn't always easy. Nothing has been easy for so long, since papa died really, that I don't know why I expected this to be any different.

Where did I last leave off? Oh right, I had just met them at the airport. Wow, it was so exciting to see their faces and to try to make sense of them being in this new world with me.

"Rosa, Rosa, Rosa," Mami cried over and over again. We hugged and held each other and cried for a very long time. Eventually, I caught a peek of Attorney Lily out of the corner of my eye. She had her arms crossed snugly, and she unhooked her arms to wipe a tear from her right eye, and went back to watching us, smiling while hugging her arms. At that moment I came back to reality, a little bit, still feeling like my feet were floating off the ground.

"There is someone that you have to meet," I said to my family in Spanish, and took them over to meet Attorney Lily. "She made everything possible." Attorney Lily looked a bit embarrassed at the attention,

but Mami didn't notice her reaction while she showered her with kisses, tight embraces, and thanks for bringing us together. I will remember those first moments forever, the ones when everything felt possible, when it seemed like our joy would be enough to overcome any obstacle that we ever might face. In those moments, there were no obstacles, just love. So much love.

As Mami and Maria told me about their trip, the bus rides through Argentina, the flights into America, I thought about my similar journey a few years earlier. I thought about all the things that had happened since, all that I wish I could take back. I wished that I could rewind time, put us all on those planes and buses and have them run in reverse, all the way back to Jujuy, back to that classroom before Señora Cuenca entered our world, when Ana and I dreamed of living next door to each other, and I was going be a teacher, and our children would have played together. Those dreams are gone now; no turning back, just moving on.

The second best thing that happened after reuniting with Mami and Maria was being able to finally move out of the shelter. Attorney Lily's friend had given us her house. Can you believe such a thing? To give someone a house? Although I know there are some very bad people in America, like the Cuencas, there are also the Attorney Lilys and her friends, the kinds of people who give you a house because they know you really need a place to live. Well, it would have been impossible for Mami and Maria to join me to live in the shelter, but we certainly did not need a house as nice and big as the one we were given. You should have seen the look on Mami's face when she saw that we had an indoor washer and dryer. After Attorney Lily drove us back to town, she took us to our new place, and Mami just stood at the front door for a long time, in disbelief that such a grand place was ours. It has big windows in front, and central air conditioning, and three bedrooms, one for each of us. Back in Jujuy, no one, except maybe the high government people, lived in such an extravagant way.

Mami stood on the front stoop and wept until I hugged her and hugged her and brought her inside. She walked in and out of every room, shocked and thrilled. She opened the refrigerator and freezer and took in the cold blast of air, I bet imagining all of the cooking that she could do for her daughters. She pressed the button to start the microwave, never having seen one before, and then laughed like a child as she pressed all of the buttons on the front, looking down, guiltily, and then around to see if anyone was watching. "Sorry," she said to Attorney Lily, when she realized that she was not alone in the room. Mami smiled, "Increíble, no?" She happily looked up at Attorney Lily and reached to give her a kiss on the cheek. Attorney Lily agreed, "Increíble," she repeated.

As overwhelmed as Mami was by every detail of our new house, Maria was equally unimpressed. She wasn't particularly nice or talkative to Attorney Lily when she tried talking to her about Hiawassee Springs, or her new school, or what it was she liked to do for fun so that Attorney Lily could make sure that she found clubs or activities that she might enjoy for the summer before school started again in the fall. Maria just stared out the window of the car, giving her nothing more than one word answers. It wasn't until later that night, when Attorney Lily was long gone and Mami had fallen asleep in her room, exhausted from the travel and everything else, that I finally had some time alone with my sister.

"Maria," I said, "You can't possibly know how wonderful it is to finally have you here." I reached for her hand to hold and she withdrew it from me.

"As if I had a choice," she muttered, under her breath.

I was stunned. Never, not even for a minute, had I realized that

Maria might not want to come to America. Ana and I had jumped at the chance; I just assumed Maria would want this as well. I realized, then, that she must blame me, the older sister who made her leave her world. She was resentful, and didn't want Mami to know, and so she would save her resentment for me, especially when we were alone.

"Oh Maria, I didn't realize that you wouldn't . . ." I trailed off. I suddenly felt so terribly selfish for making her come to be with me, especially since it didn't seem like she wanted to be here at all.

"That I wouldn't what?" Maria fired back, eyes full of anger, "That I wouldn't want to leave my whole life back home to come to a place where I can't speak the language, that I wouldn't want to leave my friends and my school and my boyfriend and every last thing that matters to me to come to a place where my sister decided to go a while ago and then we never heard from you, to this place where Ana came and died?" Maria was full of fury and she started to cry, big heaving sobs into her hands and she sunk deeper into the sky blue covered comforter. I realized that Maria said that last bit about Ana to hurt me, to make me feel responsible. Well, I had been dealing with feeling responsible for Ana for some time now, and now I would have to add feeling responsible for Maria's unhappiness to the list of the things I had done wrong that ended up hurting other people. I wanted it to be the shortest list in the world, but it was getting long, and I always had something to tell the priests at confession.

That first conversation between Maria and me was only the beginning of some rough times to come. Mami, thank goodness, was so grateful that we were all together again that she was eager to please and excited to do whatever she could to become American. She signed up for English classes, and despite never having been formally schooled, she was getting pretty good at speaking in English. She got a few jobs cleaning some office buildings and private homes through Attorney

Lily's connections with community people, and she felt proud to be making enough money to buy us the food that we needed, and occasionally even a chocolate bar to share.

Maria, on the other hand, is still struggling very hard with everything. Although she started school for speakers of English as a second language this summer, she wasn't focused on her classes and didn't learn as fast as Mami. When it came time to enroll her in school this fall, we had to place her three grades below her age level, which made her very angry, and she didn't like spending her day with "babies." To rebel, she started hanging out with some kids from the high school, who were too old for her, and got herself into smoking cigarettes and sometimes marijuana, drinking alcohol, and basically finding all kinds of trouble for herself. After the second time I heard Maria sneak back into her window close to midnight, on a school night, I decided to have a talk with her.

"Maria, what are you doing?" I asked, when she had one foot in and one still out of the door.

"Aren't you the smart one in the family, Rosa? I am sneaking back inside, what does it look like I'm doing?" Maria had not an ounce of remorse in her voice.

"I mean why, Maria. I can see what you are doing, but it's hurting you, and it's hurting me, and it would hurt Mami if she knew. I want better for you. Do you need some help with your English? Your classes? What can I do?" I tried to reason with her.

"As if you could do anything to 'help.' I've had enough of your 'help' already Rosa. I'm here, aren't I? What else do you want from me?" Maria was so angry, and I didn't want to make it worse, but I felt like maybe it was time to tell Maria the truth.

"Maria, I know you are angry, and I know you blame me, and I understand. Maybe you think I just selfishly wanted you to come and be with me, that I felt like I was too good to come back or something. I need you to know why you are here. I need you to understand . . ."

For the next few hours I told Maria everything. I thought about holding back, thinking maybe she was too young to know, but I decided against it. It was time. I told her about the Cuencas, Martin and Ana, and Marco. I told her about the things I did and that I needed her and Mami here to keep them safe. I tried to make her understand. I could feel some of her anger soften with surprise at my story, but at least a partial wall remained. She agreed that we didn't need to tell Mami what I had told her. She agreed to try to make things work in America before taking off back home like she wanted to. I agreed to give her the freedom to hate it, to resent that she didn't have control over her life like she wanted.

The next day in school I was exhausted from my night with Maria. I felt a weight lifted off my chest, though, having shared my story with her. I talked to Philip during lunch, and before we were supposed to head to our next shared class, I reached up and kissed him on the cheek. He flushed bright red and touched his hand to the kissed cheek.

"Rosie, what was that for?" He could barely get the words out from behind his big, white smile.

"For being you, Philip. Thanks." I smiled at him, and then ran into the girls' bathroom to catch my breath before our next class, amazed at my boldness. If Maria could try to make this work, then I could try, too.

Doing my best,
Rosa

Chapter 43

Mila

I woke, several hours later, from that rum induced haze, face down on the cool, hard floor and heaved into the trash bin. At some point during the night I had at least had the good sense to find a garbage bag to put in the bin so that I wasn't making a mess all over my room. I had already made such a mess of things.

A girl. This was not supposed to happen. I was not supposed to get pregnant, but if I did, I always promised myself that things would be different for me than they were for my mom. I had pictured how it would all go, very much the Hollywood story, like Reese Witherspoon and Ryan Phillipe and their two tow-headed beautiful kids. My kids would come with me to my red carpet premiers, when they were old enough, of course. We would be dressed up with jewels and gowns in all of the latest fashions, and we would wave at all of the paparazzi who were just dying to get pictures of our amazingly beautiful family. I would feign annoyance, but really, I wouldn't mind that all of those people were just dying to get a look at me, at us. Until our children were old enough, my husband and I would go just the two of us to my film events and all of the award ceremonies, and we would have a nanny that would look after the children, or maybe their grandmother would come from Slovakia to look after them and teach them my native language, exotic and exciting to their perfect and beautiful little ears.

I heard Reese and her very cute husband got divorced. But now Reese has another famous actor boyfriend, and he really likes her kids, so things worked out fine for them, too. I need my own Hollywood ending, but I am not sure how to find it here. I mean, I try my best, but how could I bring Hollywood to Bratislava or Hiawassee Springs or any other hole in the wall in Nowheresville, USA or Slovakia for that matter. I looked up at my bed longingly, wishing that I had the energy to crawl back up there. I was stuck on the floor. My head pounded and the room spun. I really had hit the bottom.

Okay, Mila, time to pull yourself together. I still have my looks, until my baby makes me all fat and gross, and I am still a great actress. So what if my mom won't talk to me? Who needs her? I still had Attorney Lily looking into civil fees we could get from Chico and all those other jerks. So, even if my Attorney seems like she has a pole stuck up her you know what, I'm sure she'd still give me the money if any came my way. I worked and worked and worked at that stupid restaurant and then at that stupid club, and I have nothing to show for it. Those jerk men owe me and I hope they pay up soon.

As soon as the room finally stopped swirling I came to some clarity on my life: it was time to go. Okay, Mila. Now, think think think. New York City or Hollywood? I needed to pick one. I needed some money and I needed a plan. As I continued to think about which city would make me a star faster, I also tried to get up from the floor. Neither activity was proving successful. Just as I got both hands on the bed for the last push upwards, the phone rang. I looked down and saw the glowing green light of the display coming from the ground. I slumped back down and answered it.

"Hello?" I tried to sound normal when I answered. What in the world was normal anymore? I tried at least to sound like someone that wasn't hung over, pregnant, and lying on the floor. I guess that was a start.

"Mila, it's me." It was my mother. I hadn't heard a word from her in months.

"Oh," I said, not knowing what else to say.

"Oh?" she said, angrily, in a mocking tone. "Is that all you have to say for yourself, all you have to say to your mother? We have not spoken in months."

"Sorry, mama, I am tired." It even sounded lame to my ears, but I had thought about talking to my mother every day for these last few months, hoping that she would call me, and now that she had, I really had no idea what to say to her.

"You're tired? I've been up all night working a double shift and you're tired? Oh goodness, Mila." Mama then said an expression that is the Slovak equivalent to "youth is wasted on the young." It still wasn't getting us anywhere.

"Anyway," mama continued, "I kept waiting for the phone to ring, hoping that you would tell me that you had gotten rid of it. So, Mila, did you?" I gulped, too exhausted for a fight with mama, but stunned that we hadn't spoken because she was waiting for me to call her. Me call her? Wasn't she the one that hung up on me the last time we talked? And "get rid of it"? Seriously. This wasn't an "it," this was my baby we were talking about. This was the baby girl I didn't necessarily plan for, but didn't think I would "get rid of" either. When did I become so indignant about this baby? I couldn't even keep track of my feelings from one minute to the next. The doctor told me this might happen. It must be the hormones.

"Mila, are you there? Can you hear me?" My thoughts ran round and round in circles and still I didn't feel like I could talk to my mother. Did I "get rid of it?" What kind of thing was that to say to me? I did the only thing I could think of at the time to avoid a fight with mama, but to stall for an answer.

"Hello, hello?" I said into the receiver, pretending not to hear my mother's voice on the other end, when clearly I could. I could hear her saying my name, over and over again. I hung up the phone, slumped back down on the floor and cried.

I'm not sure how much time passed, but the phone rang again later, it still seemed light outside, and I still didn't have any good answers.

"Hello?" I said, into the receiver, half ready to pretend again that the connection was bad and to hang up on my mother.

"Hi, Mila, it's me. Attorney Lily. I have some new information in your case. Can I come over? Or maybe you'd like me to pick you up and we can go for some tea at Mabel's?"

Hmmm … getting out of the house. Seemed overwhelming and too difficult, but Lily really sounded like she was trying to be nice, not like the last time I saw her during my doctor's appointment.

"Sure sure. I can be ready in about twenty minutes," I ventured, feeling like even that was optimistic.

"I can be there in thirty minutes. I'll honk and meet you outside, okay?" She sounded chipper. I was hoping that this good news meant lots of money for me.

"Sounds cool. I will be ready for you." We hung up and I started my effort to remove myself from the floor in earnest. I took a hot shower, always a good hangover remedy, dressed in the only clothes that seemed to still cover my belly, even though I couldn't button my pants anymore. Before I knew it, I heard the honk and out I went. I opened the door of Attorney Lily's car and slid inside, with more grace than I felt I could possess at the time. I really was a good actress.

We drove to Mabel's, a local coffee shop, to discuss my case, eat some pie, drink some coffee. Attorney Lily made me drink decaf, since she heard that caffeine was bad for the baby. I wonder what she'd think of the bottle of rum I downed last night. Caffeine had to be a very easy ride for my baby's little digestive system after that.

"So, Mila. I've got some really good news. The judge has accepted our civil suit against Chico, Carlos, Rodrigo and their crew, and we've been able to seize many of their assets." She looked at me expectantly, like I should understand what in the world she was talking about.

"Um, Attorney Lily, I think either my English isn't good enough yet or you are speaking lawyer talk." I tried to be cute about it, but I hated when I didn't understand something and I couldn't just pretend like I did.

"Oh, sorry, Mila, I'm just really excited about this. Basically, you might be able to receive lots of money, and all you would need to do is go back to court and testify …"

"Again?" I said, suddenly sick to my stomach. It could have been the baby, or that rum, but the idea of having to sit in a courtroom again and look at Chico's face, and Carlos, and have them see me pregnant like this, and maybe they would think that it's their baby, and, just the idea of it was making me sick. "No, no, Attorney Lily, I'm sorry, I can't do it. I do need money, though. My funds are running out and no more checks are coming. Do you think you could help me find a job? I'll do whatever. I have waitress experience and I could also clean offices or houses. You must have friends that could use my services."

"Mila, I understand why you are apprehensive about seeing Chico and Carlos again, and I promise I wouldn't ask you to do this unless I felt like it was really good for your case." I cut her off. I was so angry.

"My case? My case? What about what's good for me? And my life? Is that all you care about, *Attorney* Lily, my case?" I spat the word "attorney" at her, looking for some reaction. I saw sadness in her eyes and heard heaviness in her voice. She waited a few minutes, took a deep breath and responded, but she never raised her voice at me.

"Okay, Mila. I know you've got a lot on your plate. We can talk about this later. Want to order a piece of pie? Looks like they've got peach today. Have you ever tried peach pie? It's a local specialty. Let me get you a slice." Lily was trying. Hard. I decided to back off. Of course I'd tasted peach pie, but I pretended that it was my first time for her. I ate some pie, we drank our coffees, and she took me back to the shelter. I collapsed on the bed, exhausted from the conversations with my mother and with Attorney Lily, but feeling – finally – an actual bit of clarity.

I needed to get out of the shelter. I needed to make some money. I needed to give this baby a better life than the one I had made for myself.

I put up advertisements all over town for anyone looking for a cleaning person and I found a few offices, and a couple of restaurants that paid me by the hour to clean. For the next few months, I worked, I slept, and my belly grew. Attorney Lily took me to my appointments for the baby, and even though she didn't seem to understand why I wouldn't do the whole civil trial option when the money would have been really helpful, we otherwise seemed to get along fine. I saved up enough money for a bus ticket that would get me to Texas. I had seen the maps and it seemed like Texas was at least halfway to California. I didn't do anything stupid – like drink a bottle of rum or call Ty – again, but I did feel less and less connected to the baby. I knew that she deserved better than I could give her right now, and I decided to give her the best.

My baby girl was born on December 2nd. I named her Anna, after Rosa's friend that I had heard so much about, and called her "Ani," which means "very beautiful" in Slovak, my language. She was really very beautiful. By the 4th, I was home from the hospital. By the 5th, I had left Ani on the shelter's stoop, with this message:

> Dear Attorney Lily,
> Thank you for everything that you do for me, but I have to make my way. Please see that Anna finds a good home.
> Love,
> Mila.

I knew that Attorney Lily would take care of Ani, and make sure that she had a better childhood than I could provide. I was only twenty years old, and I had my whole life in front of me. Now, Anna could have hers, too.

Lily (Conclusion)

Mila had called and we had made plans to meet for an early brunch on Sunday after she came home from the hospital. I picked her up at 10, but when I got to the shelter, I saw that the car seat we had purchased was sitting out on the stoop. "Ugh, irresponsible girl," I muttered under my breath, thinking that a car seat outside in this unseasonably wet weather could get warped from all the moisture, or bother the baby if it started to smell like mold.

As I got closer, I realized that Anna was inside the car seat, sleeping. Where in the world was Mila? When I saw my name on the note attached to Anna's blanket, I started to panic. My pulse raced out of my skin. Oh Mila, what in the world have you done?

I'm not sure why I decided to read the note rather than run inside like a crazy person trying to find Mila, but that is what I did. Once I read the note, and realized that Mila had left Anna in my care, I was dumbfounded. I took the baby inside, careful not to wake her while she slept peacefully in her car seat, and searched around the shelter for Mila. I knew it in my gut, but the emptiness of her shelter room confirmed for me one stunning fact: Mila was gone. I called her cell phone and heard an automated message that the number had been disconnected. My mind started to spin. Think, Lily. Think. I buckled Anna into the middle backseat of my car, just like they had showed us how to do at the hospital after Mila had the baby, and I drove to the bus station. No Mila. I decided to try the airport, even though it would take an hour to get there.

On the way there, I tried to focus on the road, and somewhere on the way to Tallahassee, Anna started to cry. "What's wrong, baby?" I asked, in the most nurturing voice I could muster. I realized at that point, that Anna was either hungry or cold or wet and soiled, and that she probably hadn't eaten in God knows how many hours. I detoured from the airport and found the nearest store that sold baby formula. I bought a bottle, mixed the formula at the store with the drinking fountain water, and fed her while sitting on a bench inside, too tired and confused to head back to the car.

Eventually, I made it to the airport. Unsurprisingly, still no Mila. I knew that the father of the baby was named "Ty," and I probably could have called around until I spoke to every "Ty" in Hiawassee Springs. As I drove back to my house, I thought about what to do next, how I would explain the situation to Josh, how I could find Mila, and whether to give her baby to the Department of Children and Families to put up for adoption. I ran over all the possible endings to Anna's story in my head, but my heart said one thing: this is your baby, Lily. You wanted some direction and you might one day want the chance to have a baby, well here she is. I became Anna's mother on that drive. Somewhere in between Tallahassee and Hiawassee Springs, I became the mother that Mila had counted on me to become.[67]

I came home and tried to explain it all to Josh. He wasn't happy and he didn't understand. He took out his tattered grey duffel bag and started to pack his things.

"Josh, where in the world are you going?" I was honestly confused by his response. I mean, he was the one who had wanted a baby even more than I had.

"Lily, this is too much. You don't even realize that your allegiances are all wrong. What about our marriage? Now you are adopting your client's baby? Were you even going to ask my opinion?" His voice was laced with sadness, disappointment, and thinly veiled anger.

I wanted to reply, "Of course I thought of you, Josh." I wanted that to be the truth. Really, though, I knew that he was right, that I didn't care what his opinion was about the whole matter. I knew from that car ride on that I would raise Anna with or without his help.

Josh left our house. It is a very small town, and I see him often. For a while, he would pretend like he hadn't noticed me, his eyes fol-

---

67. Lest you think I turned into a total maniac and just stole the baby, fear not. Soon after all of this transpired I contacted my close friend Claire who works as an adoption attorney in Orlando and made sure that I would not be accused of kidnapping the child. I jumped through every last hoop and dotted every "I" to make sure that Anna was legally my daughter.

lowing me while he pretended to be engrossed in a conversation with Charlie, the produce guy. Lately, slowly, he has come around, and last week, he called and invited me for coffee.

I walked over to Mabel's, where the coffee is halfway decent, but the gossip is always cooking. As I peered through the smudged glass on the door I could see that Josh had already arrived, shaggy hair and slim shoulders slumped over his book. "Same old Josh," I thought to myself, surprised and saddened that I didn't feel much of anything when I looked at him.

I opened the door, struggling slightly to enter the small frame with Anna nestled in a green sling on my body, looking every bit the pea in a pod. Josh looked up, and noticeably brightened until his eyes glanced downward, seeing my human pouch.

"I didn't realize that you were bringing the baby." He stood up and awkwardly leaned in to kiss me on the cheek, almost smushing Anna in the process. I deftly avoided the impending squish, and moved the front of the sling so that Josh could see Anna's little face. I opened one of her clenched fists and pretended to extend it to Josh. "Pleased to meet you, Professor Stone," acting as if I were Anna at her most formal.

Josh, after pausing for a second, decided to play along. "Yes, Anna, great to meet you, too. I've heard great things about your work." Josh did his best, but I didn't marry him for his sense of humor. We proceeded to sit, talk, and drink coffee.[68] I told him about having hired a family lawyer and recently finalizing the adoption. Josh did not offer congratulations.

"So, she's yours now, officially?" he asked.

"Yes, name changed and all."

"Anna Stone?"

"No, Josh. Anna Walker, like her mom." I said the last sentence slowly, and with as much kindness as I could muster. Josh and I had

---

68. I ordered an iced coffee instead of the hot variety which I prefer, in case I accidentally spilled some on the baby I was "wearing." The sling I have came with an informational DVD which teaches you that the sling can be worn almost all the time, but you can never 1) prepare or consume hot beverages while baby-wearing or 2) wear the baby in the car while the vehicle is in motion.

separated, but we hadn't talked about anything official yet, like name changes or divorce. "Josh, I am going to change my last name back to Walker, once we've finalized..."

"So, that's it, Lily? It's over, and I don't even get a say?" He looked equal parts sad and combative. I tried to be gentle.

"I'm so sorry, Josh, for everything. And I'm grateful to you, for bringing me to this place, for giving me wings to try something new, and for all the unpredictable experiences that have followed ..." I reached across the table to take his hands in mine, but he pulled them away and folded his arms defiantly instead. I took a breath and tried again, "Josh, my life is going in a different direction now, and Anna and me, well, we have to forge our own path. I hope, with time ..."

"You hope what, Lily?" Josh had venom in his voice and tears in his eyes, "You hope we can still be *friends*? Please don't even ..." Josh grabbed his hooded grey sweatshirt from the back of his chair and fled the diner, wiping his eyes with his forearm on his way out.

Mabel's diner didn't have one of those handy-dandy fixtures that stop a door from slamming, which Josh probably appreciated, given the mood he was in, but the door woke Anna screaming from her peaceful sleep. As I bounced in place trying to in vain to calm her, I realized that this was it, ready or not. Today was the first day of the rest of my life, and Anna and I were officially a team, ready to take on the world. Eventually. At the moment, I felt tired to my bones from the run-in with Josh, which ended far less amicably than I had hoped.

"Okay, Anna, enough drama for one day, right?" I looked at her sweet face and bounced her against my body. "How about we head to Tia Rosa's for some delicious empanadas?" Anna didn't answer, because, well, she's a baby, so I buckled her into her car seat and stared at the poorly paved road stretching for miles ahead of us. I exhaled and started the engine. Until Anna starts on solid food, I'll just have to eat for two.

Afterword

from the author

As far as my clients are concerned, this is our story. Normally, in the name of professional ethics and client confidentiality, I couldn't (and wouldn't) tell you about my clients. I wouldn't tell you their names, let alone their stories. In this particular case, Rosa and Mila are composite characters embodying many of the stories I have heard while practicing humanitarian immigration law. I wanted you to know about them, so that hopefully other girls and women would not have to suffer the same fate. Women all over the world – even in the United States, even in these modern times – still do not have complete agency over their own lives.

I, selfishly, wanted you to know a bit about my story, which has much – but not all – in common with Attorney Lily, so that if you are one of those lucky people who has the luxury to spend many years focused on higher education, you will think about law school, and you will consider spending your life as an advocate for those whose voices have been taken from them. I wouldn't be half the attorney, or person, that I am today without having met people like "Rosa" and "Mila," and so many of my other clients, whose stories I can't share with you. I am grateful to all my clients for the invaluable lessons they have taught me by opening my eyes to courage and resilience, to a new perspective on the world and our increasing interconnectedness and interdependence.

"Rosa" and "Mila" are two women who might, and likely do, live somewhere in your community. Everyone who took the time to read this book cares at least enough to know about one form of human exploitation, and possibly to play a role. If anyone had reached out to these two women during their years of exploitative labor and hardship, they might not have suffered as long as they did. It would only have taken one person to see their sadness and say something – one patron at a restaurant, one neighbor on the street. It would only have taken one person. But the silence of good people everywhere lets trafficking happen.